The Anthem
in New England
before 1800

Da Capo Press Music Reprint Series

MUSIC EDITOR
BEA FRIEDLAND
Ph.D., City University of New York

The Anthem

in New England

before 1800

RALPH T. DANIEL

DA CAPO PRESS · NEW YORK · 1979

Library of Congress Cataloging in Publication Data

Daniel, Ralph T
    The anthem in New England before 1800.

    (Da Capo Press music reprint series)
    Reprint of the ed. published by Northwestern Univer-
sity Press, Evanston, Ill., in series: Pi Kappa Lambda
studies in American music.
    "Musical supplement": p.
    Bibliography: p.
    Includes index.
    1. Church music — New England — History and criticism.
I. Title.
[ML2911.D35 1979]   783.4'0974   78-31121
ISBN 0-306-79511-6

This Da Capo Press edition of *The Anthem in New England
Before 1800* is an unabridged republication of the first
edition published in Evanston, Illinois in 1966 with
the exception of a few minor emendations by the author.
It is reprinted by arrangement with
Northwestern University Press.

Published by Da Capo Press, Inc.
A Subsidiary of Plenum Publishing Corporation
227 West 17th Street, New York, N.Y. 10011

The Anthem in New England before 1800

 Pɪ Kᴀᴘᴘᴀ Lᴀᴍʙᴅᴀ Studies in American Music

The Anthem

in New England

before 1800

RALPH T. DANIEL

Northwestern University Press · *Evanston* · 1966

PLATE I, from *The Book of Psalms* by Henry Ainsworth (Amsterdam, 1612), is reproduced by courtesy of The Houghton Library, Harvard University.

PLATE II, from *The Whole Booke of Psalmes* by Thomas Ravenscroft (London, 1621), is reproduced by permission of The Huntingdon Library, San Marino, California.

For Genevieve

Foreword

THE SOCIETY OF PI KAPPA LAMBDA was organized in 1918 with the goal of serving as a means for stimulation of the scholarly approach to the study of music. A student who is particularly gifted as a public performer automatically receives recognition; but the individual who is more inclined toward the study of music as an intellectual discipline than as preparation for concert presentation has been too frequently ignored as a significant figure in the musical scene. It was for throwing light on the importance of intellectual and academic accomplishments that the Society was founded.

Through its individual chapters in various colleges, universities, and schools of music throughout the United States, Pi Kappa Lambda annually elects to membership those students who have demonstrated interest, aptitude, and outstanding achievement in the study of music with regard to its intellectual aspects together with those qualities essential for leadership in the development of the art. Members may be elected in the junior or senior year of collegiate study, or during graduate study at either the master's or the doctoral level.

In line with its purpose of encouraging the creative approach to serious study, the Society has undertaken as a project the publication of what is anticipated as a series of studies in American music. It takes great pride in introducing, as the first in the expected series *The Anthem in New England before 1800* by Ralph Daniel.

It is hoped that this will serve to impel other scholars toward the investigation of topics particularly germane to the American cultural scene and appropriate to its musical development.

GEORGE HOWERTON
President-General
Pi Kappa Lambda

Evanston, Illinois
April 1, 1965

Preface

*For the first two hundred years the history of music in the United States
is the history of psalmody.*

THE OPENING SENTENCE quoted above from George Hood's *History of Music in New England,* the first consequential attempt to deal with the subject, has served, unfortunately, as the prototype for many similar oversimplifications since it first appeared in 1846. Discoveries during the past fifty years have shown that there was a very considerable activity in secular music; and even in the relatively circumscribed area of church music there occurred during the last half of the eighteenth century a very significant departure from the simple psalmody of the first one hundred and fifty years.

The element most important to this rapid burgeoning beginning about 1760 is that which transfers the focal point of interest from the domain of the religious historian to that of the musicologist: after nearly one hundred and fifty years of complete subservience of music to liturgical function, there appears in music intended for the church and its adjuncts the germ of an *aesthetic* impetus—the impulse to create beauty in musical terms. Certainly the primary *raison d'être* of this new music remained that of heightening the effect of religious words, but the tremendous increase in and variety of the musical resources utilized, when compared to the simple, square-cut psalm tunes, make inescapable the conclusion that, for the composer at least, a large part of the motivation was musical rather than religious.

What generated this aesthetic impulse? Where and when did it originate in the New World? In what form was it manifest? What patterns served as models for the native composers of New England? Who were the creative spirits who fostered the development of the art? What was the course of its evolution and growth? These are some of the questions which the present study seeks to answer.

The significance of this chapter previously missing from the history of music in the United States is increasingly evident when one considers that it was in the forms and geographical area with which this study is concerned that original composition by native composers first flourished. Whether Francis Hopkinson's "My Days Have Been So Wondrous Free" or James Lyon's "Ode" for the commencement exercises at Princeton in 1759 was the first composition by a native-born American will probably never be unequivocally established. Although the determination of the actual *first* is not of any real consequence, it would be gratifying, for the purposes of this essay, to know that Lyon's "Ode" preceded Hopkinson's ballad, for then primacy would fall to the type of composition dealt with in the following pages. In any event, Lyon's collection of anthems and psalm tunes, *Urania*, of 1761, is indeed a more significant production than Hopkinson's single song and antedates Hopkinson's *Collection of Psalm Tunes with a Few Anthems* by two years.

The generic classification most commonly used by late eighteenth-century composers for their decorative church music was "anthem." Designations such as "ode," "dirge," "poem," or "chorus" occurred less frequently for pieces similar in musical style to the anthems. Such works were usually intended for a specific occasion, often secular, and have been excluded from the following study because of their special nature as "occasional music."

For the composers represented in eighteenth-century New England publications, the determinative features of anthems seem to have been a through-composed plan (as distinguished from the strophic structure of psalm and hymn tunes wherein the same musical material served for more than one verse of the text), freer treatment of the scriptural prose text,[1] greater variety of texture than that employed in the basically four-part, chordal style of psalm tunes, and the incorporation of musical materials which required some degree of training and rehearsal—rhythmic, melodic, harmonic, and textural patterns too intricate for performance by the congregation. Thus, this was music to be listened to by the congregation, not only for the spiritual edifica-

---

1. At an annual convention of the Sacred Harp Singers in 1949, I asked one of the participants to distinguish between a hymn and an anthem. He replied to the effect that "in a hymn you would sing 'Hand me that pike, Jack' while in an anthem the text would be something like 'Hand me, hand me that pike, that pike, O Jack.' "

tion derived from the text, but also for the aesthetic perception implicit in any artistic performance.

Except for the few instances when they were published separately, in periodicals, or in special collections, the anthems of the eighteenth century were published in the psalm and hymn tune books designed for use in singing schools, "worshiping assemblies," and churches. Usually only a few of these longer pieces were included in one book.

Not all the anthems to be considered are by American composers. Many of the most popular selections of the period were by composers of the mother country. These imported products were very significant, and analyzing the musical style of the English models and tracing the extent of their influence upon native composers constitute a large and important segment of the following survey. The older English anthems are discussed first so that they may serve as a standard for judging the American products; and, for the sake of a perspective within which to make a valid appraisal of the later developments, the first two chapters deal, respectively, with a cursory survey of church music in New England and in England during the seventeenth and eighteenth centuries.

To Professor Otto Kinkeldey, who first called my attention to this unexplored chapter of Americana, to Professor G. Wallace Woodworth, for advice in its early stages, and to the staffs of Houghton and Widener Libraries at Harvard University, the Music Department of the Boston Public Library, the Congregational Library and the libraries of the American Antiquarian Society, the Massachusetts Historical Society, and the Harvard Musical Association go my sincere thanks.

RALPH T. DANIEL

Contents

Tables and Figures

The Anthem in New England before 1800

I

Church Music in New England before 1760

I T IS QUITE PROBABLE that when the little band of Pilgrims landed at Plymouth on a blustery December day in 1620 one of their first corporate acts was the singing of a psalm of thanksgiving. Although none of those who kept a chronicle of the voyage has recorded their first worship service on land—the diarists were understandably occupied with battles against the elements and the Indians rather than with the commonplaces of daily activity—it is well known that the singing of Psalms played a large part not only in the organized church services but in their home life as well. Edward Winslow, for instance, in describing the departure of the group from Holland, reported that those

> that stayed at Leyden feasted us that were to go at our pastor's house, being large; where we refreshed ourselves, after tears, with singing of Psalms, making joyful melody in our hearts as well as with the voice, there being many of our congregation very expert in music; and indeed it was the sweetest melody that ever mine ears heard.[1]

Thus, the history of church music in New England begins with the psalmody of the Pilgrim colonists and, indeed, consists solely of the practice and development of psalmody for more than one hundred years. Nothing

1. Edward Winslow, *Hypocrasie Unmasked*, chap. xxv, quoted in Alexander Young, *Chronicles of the Pilgrim Fathers*, p. 384.

more is known about the music of the native Indians than the fact that they did sing. Governor Bradford, in an entry in his journal dated July 5, 1621, comments on "the savage's barbarous singing, (for they used to sing themselves asleep)." [2]

The only music known to have been brought to America by the Pilgrims was that contained in Henry Ainsworth's metric version of the Psalms.[3] Ainsworth's handsome *The Book of Psalms, Englished both in Prose and Meter* had been published in Amsterdam in 1612 for the group of Separatists who had fled from England to Holland early in the seventeenth century. From their ranks came the nucleus of the group who embarked upon the high adventure of 1620. The music consisted of thirty-nine monophonic psalm tunes (i.e., forty-eight, of which nine were duplicates) printed typographically in the diamond-shaped semibreves and minims of the era. (See Plate I.) Regarding the sources of the tunes, Ainsworth said:

> Tunes for the Psalms I find none set of God; so that each people is to use the most grave, decent and comfortable manner of singing that they know. . . . The singing-notes, therefore, I have most taken from our former Englished Psalms, when they will fit the measure of the verse. And for the other long verses I have taken (for the most part) the gravest and easiest tunes of the French and Dutch Psalmes.[4]

The Pilgrims' more fortunate and prosperous neighbors to the north, the Puritans of the Massachusetts Bay Colony (now Boston), brought a more impressive collection of music when they arrived in 1630. Their psalter, in the first complete English metric version by Thomas Sternhold and John Hopkins,[5] was much older than that of Ainsworth, having been completed in 1562. After successive musical editions by John Day (1562), William Damon (1579), Thomas Este (1592), and Ralph Allison (1599), the compilation destined to be transplanted in the New World was that of Thomas Ravenscroft of 1621; and a worthy seed it was. It was by far the best musical setting of its day, for it contained almost one hundred tunes set in four parts by such illustrious Englishmen as John Dowland, Giles

2. Young, *op. cit.*, p. 211.

3. For a description of the book and reprints in modern notation of all the psalm tunes, see Waldo S. Pratt, *The Music of the Pilgrims*.

4. Ainsworth, *Book of Psalms*, Preface, p. [1]. The "former Englished Psalms" probably refers either to the Sternhold and Hopkins version of 1562 or to the Scottish variant of 1564. The French psalm tunes are those of Bourgeois, Goudimel, and Le Jeune in Marot and de Beze's *Genevan Psalter* of 1562. The source of the Dutch tunes is unknown.

5. For a bibliographical history of this work and the definitive study of the group and their musical activities, see Percy Scholes, *The Puritans and Music*.

PLATE I

Pſalm. C.   353

a Preiſt, oʒ Sacrificer, is the name of the Kings cheif officer, as in 2. Sam. 8, 18. Davids ſonns were Cohens, (Cheif-rulers, Aularchai as the Greek trãnſlateth than,) which is expounded in 1. Chron. 18. 17. to be the firſt (oʒ Cheif) at the Kings hand. It hath the name of miniſtration, Iſa. 61, 6, 10. and was a title ſpecially given to Aaron and his ſonns, that miniſtred unto God in the Sanctuarie. Exo. 28. 3. 4. 41.   caled eʒ were cãing : that is prayed for the people, as Exod. 32, 11. &c. Num. 14, 17, 19. & 16, 22, 46. 1. Sam. 7. 9. & 12. 19. 23. Here upon Moſes & Samuel were not ſo foʒ cheif interceſſoʒs with God, Ier. 15, 1.   v. 7. of a clowd] as Exo. 33. 9. Num. 16, 42. and this noteth God a father, but with ſome obſcurity : and ſo is inferiour to the mediation of Chriſt, who hath without clowds oʒ ſhadowes obteyned eternal redemption foʒ us, that we may goe boldly to the throne of grace, foʒ to receiv mercy and find grace to help in time of need. Heb. 4, 14, 16. & 7, 25. & 9. 11, 12.   v. 8. a God forgiving] a mighty-God that pardoneſt, oʒ tookeſt away, to weet, the puniſhment of their ſpu: ſee Pſ. 25, 18.   and taking] oʒ though thou tookeſt vengeance.   on their practiſes] theirs that is the peoples, foʒ whom Moſes prayed, as Num. 14, 20, 21, 23. Exod. 32, 14, 34, 35. oʒ theirs, that is, Moſes and Aarons ſynns, which God puniſhed and would not be intreated, as Num. 20, 12, Deut. 3, 23, 24, 25, 26.

Pſalm. 100.

1.   A pſalm for confeſſion:
SHowt ye triumphantly to Iehovah, al the earth.

2. Serv ye Iehovah with gladnes: come before him, with ſinging-joy.

3. Know ye, that Iehovah he is God: he made us, and not wee: his people, & ſhe p of his paſture.

4. Enter ye his gates, with confeſſion; his courts with praiſe: confeſs ye to him, bleſs ye his name.

5. For Iehovah is good his mercy is for ever: & his faith, unto generation & generation.

Pſalm. 100.

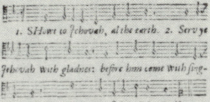

1. SHowt to Iehovah, al the earth. 2. Serv ye Iehovah with gladnes: before him come with ſing-ing-mirth. 3. Know, that Iehovah he God is:

Its he that made us, and not Wee;
his folk, and ſheep of his feeding.
4. O with confeſſion enter yee
his gates, his courtyards with praiſing:
confeſs to him, bleſs ye his name.
5. Becauſe Iehovah he good is:
his mercy ever is the ſame:
and his faith, unto al ages.

Annotations.

Verſ. 1. for confeſſion] for the publik praiſe of God, with thanks for his mercies.
v. 2. ſinging] oʒ ſhouting, ſhowting-mirth.   v. 3. made us] this woʒd is uſed both foʒ our firſt creation in nature, Gen. 1, 26. and foʒ the making of us a peeple and excellent with graces and bleſſings, as 1. Sam. 12. 6. Deut. 32, 6. Iſa. 43, 7. & 29. 23. Ephe. 2, 10.   and not we] oʒ, and his we are: as the Hebrue in the margine readeth it. Both ſenſes are good.
ſheep] oʒ flock which he feedeth. See Ezek. 34, 30, 31. Pſal. 95. 7.   v. 4. confeſſion] the ſacrifice of thanks was thus named; 2. Chron. 29, 31. Ier. 17. 26.   v. 5. faith] oʒ, faithfulnes: truth, in performing his promiſes.

Ii 3   Pſalm. CI.

Ainsworth, *The Book of Psalms*

PLATE II

Ravenscroft, *The Whole Booke of Psalmes*

Farnaby, Thomas Morley, Thomas Tallis, and Thomas Tomkins. It is generally believed, since the Puritans were so strongly influenced by the teachings and practices of John Calvin (who sanctioned only Psalms sung in unison as the music of his church), that the Boston group sang only the melodies in their organized worship services, using the more entertaining and diverting four-part settings for worship and recreation in the home. (See Plate II.)

Whether the smaller group of Puritans, who landed in Salem in 1628, used the Ainsworth or the Sternhold and Hopkins version is not known. The personal copy of Sternhold and Hopkins owned by John Endicott, leader of the Salem group, is in the library of the Massachusetts Historical Society. On the other hand, the records of the First Church in Salem report that they were using the Ainsworth version in 1667. It may be that the group adopted the Ainsworth version after their arrival.

The rather quaint versifications of Ainsworth and of Sternhold and Hopkins are poetically rather roughhewn, but it was objection to their deviations from the Hebrew original rather than to their literary defects that prompted a group of Boston ministers and scholars to produce, in 1640, *The Whole Book of Psalms faithfully translated into English Metre.* More popularly known as the *Bay Psalm Book* from its inception in the Massachusetts Bay Colony, this first New England version of the Psalms is a monumental landmark not only in music but also in other fields of American scholarship—bibliographical, typographical, historical, religious, and literary.

The inference might be drawn, from the very fact of publication by leading ministers of a new metrical version of the Psalms suitable for congregational use, that singing in the churches was generally accepted and popular. Such was not the case. Although the Puritan concept of music as the "invention of the devil" has been largely exaggerated in the past, it is true that there was sufficient controversy regarding the suitability of singing in public worship to cause a defensive tone in the Preface to the *Bay Psalm Book* and to persuade the Reverend John Cotton of Boston to publish in 1647 an essay in support of singing, *Singing of Psalms a Gospel Ordinance: Or a treatise wherein are handled these four particulars:*

> *I. Touching the duty itself.*
> *II. Touching the matter to be sung.*
> *III. Touching the singers.*
> *IV. Touching the manner of singing.*

Cotton's arguments furnish an insight into the sectarian and often petty bases of the contention. In the first section, in response to those who believed that the Scriptures intended nothing more by the word "singing" than thankfulness and joy of heart, he answers that audible singing "with a lively voyce, is an holy duty of God's Worship now in the days of the New Testament." [6] He hastens to assure his readers, however, that he does not exclude "singing with the heart."

In the second section is treated the objection to the use of the Old Testament Psalms of David in New Testament days. The proponents of this argument maintained that inspired psalms of praise by members of the congregation (the rest of the brethren "say Amen to it in the close") would be more suitable. Cotton supports David's Psalms on the grounds that they are frequently quoted in the New Testament, but he also recommends other scriptural songs as well as original psalms by the congregation.

The third section is concerned with three rather trivial matters of procedure:

1. Whether one be to sing for all the rest, the rest joyning onely in spirit, and saying Amen; or the whole Congregation?
2. Whether women, as well as men; or mēn alone?
3. Whether carnall men and Pagans may be permitted to sing with us, or Christians alone, and Church-Members? [7]

To all of these questions Cotton answers with passages of Scripture supporting the view that all should sing, although his argument for allowing women to sing is rather brief and something less than enthusiastic.

The fourth section, dealing with "the manner of singing," also poses a threefold question:

1. Whether it be lawfull to sing Psalmes in Meeter devised by men?
2. Whether in Tunes invented?
3. Whether it be lawfull in Order unto Singing, to reade the Psalme? [8]

Cotton answers, on a common-sense basis, that if it is reasonable to translate the Psalms into English so that they may be understood, then it is just as lawful to translate them into metric English. Likewise, if English *words* devised by man are used so that the meaning is understood, then there should be no objection to man-made *tunes*.

For the last point, Cotton justifies "lining-out" the Psalms on the grounds that almost any means whereby God's injunctions (e.g., to sing Psalms) are carried out are justified.

This "lining-out" of the Psalms mentioned in Cotton's closing paragraph

6. John Cotton, *Singing of Psalms a Gospel Ordinance*, p. 2.
7. *Ibid.*, pp. 37–38.
8. *Ibid.*, p. 54.

was a performance practice of our ancestors by no means so distinctive of the colonists as many earlier writers would have us believe. They frequently used a description of the practice as a rather amusing interlude in their narrations, implying that the "quaint" custom of having each line of the Psalm sung first by a deacon or precentor, then by the assembled congregation, was evidence of the musical naïveté of the immigrants.

While it is true that the practice was almost universal [9] in New England during the last half of the seventeenth century and flourished until post-Revolutionary times, it was just as common in the rural churches of the mother country to which the colonial churches must be compared rather than to the larger urban congregations of the Church of England. It is a matter of record that the Puritan "Westminster Assembly" of 1664 specifically recommended the practice for those churches whose members lacked either Psalm books or the ability to read.

Although many copies of earlier editions are extant in which the owners have inserted manuscript copies of favorite tunes, the editions of the *Bay Psalm Book* [10] before 1698 have little musical significance, since it was not until then that music—thirteen tunes in two-part settings—was included by the publisher. Beginning with the first edition, however, it was stated in the concluding "Admonition" that "the verses . . . may by sung in very neere fourty common tunes; as they are collected, out of our chief musicians, by Thomas Ravenscroft. The second kinde may be sung in three tunes . . . in our English psalme books." [11]

By the time music was incorporated into this "New England Version" of the Psalms (9th ed., 1698), some marked and surprising changes in the quality of church music had occurred. Hood's account of the deterioration, although necessarily somewhat speculative, is as reliable and concise a summary as any available:

> When the Puritans first came to their wilderness homes, they cultivated music even in their College. Their songs of praise were conducted with decorum, if not with ability; and a laudable pride, if such can be, inspired them still to improve their purity and excellence. This spirit brought out

9. The Plymouth Church Records of October 2, 1681, give an account of a meeting wherein the congregation voted to adopt the practice of lining-out. Since they retained their Ainsworth Psalters until around 1700 instead of adopting the *Bay Psalm Book*, they were probably the last group to abandon the practice of singing without interruption.

10. For a thorough bibliographical description of the *Bay Psalm Book*, see Wilberforce Eames, *A List of Editions of the "Bay Psalm Book."*

11. *The Whole Book of Psalms* (1st ed., 1640), next to last page. Does the plural use of "books" imply a varied selection of psalters, or only to multiple copies of the Ravenscroft edition of Sternhold and Hopkins?

the New England version of the Psalms, a work, as a whole, incomparably better than any version that had preceded it.

But soon after their settlement, the Colonies were disturbed by contentions and party strife. Scarcely had a score of fleet years sped their flight, before errors in doctrine came in to disturb that tranquillity for which they had sought these shores. Troubles came upon troubles in rapid succession. The genius of discord settled upon the land. There was Roger Williams, Anne Hutchinson, the Quakers, and Antinomianism, to trouble their religion; the Pequod, King Philip's, and numerous petty wars with the Indians, to alarm the land. Their charters were several times annulled and restored; and oppressive acts, leading to party strife with insurrection, and twice to open war, were passed. Witchcraft, and a host of smaller evils, came swarming over the land, like the plagues of Egypt. Then, not a trouble came upon England, that was not felt in the Colonies. Every one's thoughts were upon the evils and troubles of the day. It was an age of commotion, both in England and in the Colonies.

Music dwells not in scenes of contention; she flies the abode of anarchy and confusion, and seeks a home in the land of peace. It is there, and there only, she dispenses her blessings.

The few music-books, that had from time to time found their way into the Colonies, were rapidly decreasing; and the few they had were unlike. The cultivation of music was neglected, until in the latter part of the seventeenth century, the congregations throughout New England were rarely able to sing more than three or four tunes. The knowledge and use of notes too, had so long been neglected, that the few melodies sung, became corrupted, until no two individuals sang them alike. Every melody was "tortured and twisted," [embellished?] "as every inskillful throat saw fit," until their psalms were uttered in a medley of confused and disorderly noises, rather than in a decorous song. The Rev. Mr. Walter says of their singing, that it sounded "like five hundred different tunes roared out at the same time;" and so little attention was paid to time, that they were often one or two words apart, producing noises "so hidious and disorderly, as is bad beyond expression." The manner of singing had also become so tedious and drawling, that the same author says, "I myself have twice in one note paused to take breath." The Rev. Mr. Symmes says, in his sermon on Regular Singing: "It is with great difficulty that this part of worship is performed, and with great indecency in some congregations for want of skill. It is to be feared, singing must be wholly omitted in some places, for want of skill, if this art is not revived." [12]

It is, and always will be, impossible to establish the exact causes for the degeneration in the quality of New England church music during the

12. George Hood, *A History of Music in New England*, pp. 82–85.

seventeenth century. While it is true that "music dwells not in scenes of contention," contention was not perpetual in the period; even if it had been, the situation would not have justified the abandonment of a once-popular means of "solace and comfort." And although "the few music-books . . . were rapidly decreasing," they could have been easily replaced by imports from the mother country had there been sufficient interest. Howard suggests that deacons of questionable musical ability, who lined out the Psalms, were largely responsible.[13]

It seems more likely that the waning interest in the singing of Psalms was only a reflection of a fading religious zeal once the pressure of persecution was relieved and interest was focused upon the secular affairs of establishing and ordering a new society. That there had been diminishing activity in religious affairs is certainly evidenced by the conditions which produced the "Great Awakening" revival movement in the 1730's and the success of the Wesley-Whitefield evangelism of the next decade.

Whatever the cause of the deplorable state to which church music had descended at the beginning of the eighteenth century, it was inevitable that a reaction should occur and that some attempt should be made to remedy the situation. The activity of the clergymen to reform the musical practices of the time and their eventual success is the focal point of the story of music in New England between 1700 and 1760.

About 1720 began a period of aggression by the proponents of good music among the clergy that was remarkable in its vitality. It is difficult to visualize present-day Americans becoming so concerned about any musical affair that serious debate in the form of sermons, both oral and printed, published tracts, and essays should continue for several years. Actually, the doctrinal rather than the musical aspects of this eighteenth-century controversy were probably responsible for the vigorous participation of the clergymen. For a decade after the Reverend Thomas Symmes's *The Reasonableness of Regular Singing* appeared in 1720 there waxed a "war" of tracts *pro* and *contra* learning to read music, a controversy resembling somewhat the *Guerre des Bouffons* in Paris some thirty years later.[14] The *pro* essays outnumbered the

13. John T. Howard, *Our American Music*, p. 11.

14. The inflammatory nature of the controversy is revealed by the two following excerpts from the *New England Courant*, a newspaper published in Boston. The first is dated September 16, 1723; the second, December 9, 1723.

"Last week a Council of Churches was held at the South part of Braintree, to regulate the disorders occasioned by regular [i.e., without lining-out] singing in that place, Mr. Niles, the minister having suspended seven or eight of the church for persisting in their singing by rule, contrary, as he apprehended, to the result of a former Council; but the suspended bretheren are restored to communion, their suspension declared unjust, and the

contra by a considerable percentage, of course. The learned pastors who had both the ability to write and the means to publish, and who supported musical reform almost unanimously, quite naturally would produce more than the negative, overconservative spirits who opposed the needed reform. The views of the conservatives, consequently, must be largely discerned from the statements to which the ministers gave rebuttal.

Following Symmes's pamphlet named above, most of the printed material dealing with the matter appeared between 1720 and 1730, although sporadic outbursts occurred throughout the century. The list below is a representative sampling:

Cotton Mather, *The Accomplished Singer* (1721)
Thomas Symmes, *Prejudice in Matters of Religion* (1722)
Peter Thacher, *et al.*, *Cases of Conscience about Singing Psalms* (1722)
Thomas Symmes, *Utile Dulci; or Joco-Serious Dialogue* (1723)
Cotton Mather, *A Pacificatory Letter* (1723)
Josiah Dwight, *An Essay to Silence the Outcry* (1725)
Valentine Wightman, *A Letter to the Elders* (1725)
Nathaniel Chauncey, *Regular Singing Defended* (1727)

Description of and quotation from these essays are readily available in the larger histories of music in the United States. For purposes of this brief survey it is sufficient to summarize the principal objections to reform as extracted from the various tracts by Hood:

1. That it [reading rather than lining-out the music] was a new way;— an unknown tongue.
2. That it was not so melodious as the usual way.
3. That there were so many tunes, one could never learn them.
4. That the new way made disturbance in churches, grieved good men, exasperated them and caused them to behave disorderly.
5. That it was popish.
6. That it would introduce instruments.

---

congregation ordered to sing by Rote and by Rule alternately for the satisfaction of both parties."

"We have advice from the South part of Braintree, that on Sunday the first instant, Mr. Niles, the minister of that place, performed the duties of the day at his dwelling-house, among those of the congregation who are opposers of regular singing. The regular singers met together at the meeting-house and sent for Mr. Niles, who refused to come unless they would first promise not to sing regularly; whereupon they concluded to edify themselves by the assistance of one of the Deacons who at their desire prayed with them, read a sermon, etc."

7. That the names of the notes were blasphemous.
8. That it was needless, the old way being good enough.
9. That it was only a contrivance to get money.
10. That it required too much time to learn it, made the young disorderly, and kept them from the proper influence of the family.[15]

To such objections were Symmes's answers directed in his essay, *The Reasonableness of Regular Singing, or Singing By Note:*

> I shall now proceed in the plainest most easy and popular Way I can, (for 'tis for the sake of the common People I write) to shew, That *Singing by, or according to Note,* is to be preferred to the *Usual Way of Singing,* which may be evidenced by several Arguments.
>
> 1. The first *Argument* may be taken from the *ANTIQUITY of Regular Singing. Singing by Note* is the most *Ancient Way* of singing, and claims the Preference to the other on that Account. Truth is older than Error; and is venerable for its Antiquity; but as for Error, the ancienter it is, the worse it is. There are many bad *Old Ways.* Antiquity is no infallible mark of Truth. Math. 5. 21.[16] Yet the Argument may be of Service here, because those who plead against Singing by Note, urge with much zeal and warmth, that this is a *New Way,* and the *Usual Way* is *the good Old Way,* as they call it. Here I shall endeavor to prove their Mistake; and I suppose, that if they could be convinced, that *Singing by Note* was known to, and approved of, by the first settlers of *New-England,* it would satisfy most of them as to this Point. . . . For,
>
> I. It was studied, known and approved of in our *College,* for many years after its first Founding. This is evident from the Musical *Theses* which were formerly Printed, and from some Writings containing some *Tunes,* with Directions for *Singing by Note,* as they are now Sung; and these are yet in Being, tho' of more than *Sixty Years* standing; [17] besides no Man that Studied *Musick,* as it is treated of by Alsted, Playford and others, could be ignorant of it.[18]
>
> .   .   .   .
>
> IV. *If Singing by Note is most agreeable to SCRIPTURE PRECEPT AND PATTERN, then it is better than the* Vulgar *or* Usual *Way; but Singing by Note or Rule is so;* Therefore, Singing with *Skill* or by *Note*

---

15. Hood, *op. cit.,* pp. 86–87.

16. All these essays are, in the manner of the period, liberally sprinkled with references to supporting scriptural passages.

17. These theses were lost in the tragic fire which destroyed completely the Harvard College Library in 1764. Knowledge of the nature and extent of musical instruction at the College during the seventeenth century would be invaluable for American musical scholarship.

18. Symmes, *op. cit.,* pp. 5–6.

which is the same thing, is most agreeable to the General Instructions which we have in Scripture, about the *External* part of singing. Singing by *Note* agrees best with that Direction, *Play skillfully* Ps. 33. 3. . . .[19]

It is worthy of note that the whole controversy revolved around the question of singing by "rule" versus the "regular way" (i.e., lining-out), and is, consequently, an evidence of the universality of the old custom.

The agitation for reform by the ministers would have been to little avail had the music books available for church use been limited to the *Bay Psalm Book* with its few, badly printed tunes in two parts, or to the (by then) few remaining tattered copies of Ravenscroft or to the expensive English imports. Consequently, the principal share of the credit for the reform goes to two Massachusetts ministers, John Tufts of Newburyport and Thomas Walter of Roxbury, who provided not only a direct incentive for the improvement of singing, but the means by which that improvement could be brought about.

About 1721 Tufts published his *A Very Plain and Easy Introduction to the Whole Art of Singing Psalm Tunes,*[20] the first instruction book on singing compiled in the Colonies. After five pages of "Introduction to the singing of Psalm Tunes," in which the method of notation is explained, there follow thirty-seven tunes (probably copied from Playford's *Whole Book of Psalms,* 1677) harmonized in three parts ("Cantus, Medius and Base") with letters signifying the applicable *sol-fa* syllables placed upon the staff rather than notes.

A few years later, in 1721, when the controversy regarding singing was just beginning to flourish, the Reverend Thomas Walter brought out *The Grounds and Rules of Musick explained: Or an Introduction to the Art of Singing by Note: Fitted to the meanest capacities,* which contained the first real music printed in the Colonies except for that in the *Bay Psalm Book,* and the very first to utilize bar lines. This book went through many editions before the last one in 1764. Such longevity is evidence that, along with Tufts' work, it determined the style of church music until supplanted by the publications of Josiah Flagg, Daniel Bailey, William Billings, and others in the 1760's and 1770's. There were several English publications (e.g., Brady and Tate, *New Version of the Psalms,* 1696; and Watts, *Psalms of David,* 1719, and *Hymns,* 1711) which gained a large measure of popular-

19. *Ibid.*, p. 12.
20. See Irving Lowens, "John Tuft's *Introduction to the Singing of Psalm-Tunes* (1721-1744): The First American Music Textbook" in his *Music and Musicians in Early America.*

ity throughout the eighteenth century, but well-known tunes served for these new translations and new poems.

It was with such weapons as these that the reformers won over the majority of churchgoers to the progressive point of view. But the means by which the victory was really established is revealed in the formation of singing schools.[21] The singing-school movement in the Colonies, like the cultivation of the anthem, was one of the most fruitful undertakings in eighteenth-century musical activity, and one without which the developments of the latter part of the century would have been impossible.

Symmes, in both *The Reasonableness of Regular Singing* and *Utile Dulci*, implies that there was some source of musical instruction besides that in the college during the seventeenth century; and the Reverend Mr. John Elliot, who, in 1661, translated the Psalms into Indian verse, had obviously followed some organized form of instruction in teaching the Indians to sing. The Reverend Increase Mather, in a published letter to the governor of the Corporation for Propagating the Gospel among the Indians, speaks of their "Excellent Singing of Psalms, with most ravishing Melody." [22]

But the first formally organized instruction in singing of which evidence is extant took place about 1720 in Boston.[23] In a diary entry dated March 16, 1720, The Reverend Samuel Sewall records a meeting of what must have been one of the first singing schools:

> At night Dr. Mather preaches in the School-House to the young musicians from Rev. 14.3—no man could learn that Song. House was full, and the singing extraordinarily Excellent, such as has hardly been heard before in Boston.[24]

Following quickly the example set by Boston, other communities also established musical instruction—Roxbury, Dorchester, Cambridge, Taunton, Bridgewater, Charlestown, Ipswich, Newbury, Andover, and Bradford.

These were not "schools" in the academic sense of the term, of course. They were usually conducted by a singer of some repute whom the church

21. See Alan Clark Buechner, "Yankee Singing Schools and the Golden Age of Choral Music in New England, 1760–1800."

22. Mather, *A Letter; about the Present State of Christianity among the Christianized Indians of New-England*, p. 9.

23. In the *Massachusetts Historical Society Collections*, ser. 2, IV, 30, is an account of Mr. Timothy Burbank, who died in Plymouth, October 13, 1793, aged ninety. Mr. Burbank always claimed that he attended the first singing school which introduced singing by notes at Boston.

24. Samuel Sewall, Diary, *Collections of the Massachusetts Historical Society*, ser. 5, VII, 285.

fathers saw fit to subsidize and to "call" into the community for a period of weeks or months. The two or three evening meetings each week (usually from five-thirty until eight o'clock) must have been partly in the nature of a social gathering, especially for the young people, and this extra-musical sociability may have been a powerful determinant in the success of the whole venture.

From the singing schools there gradually evolved the institution of the church choir, which, as Howard says, "grew into something more than [the ministers] had bargained for." It was natural that the best singers, unified by their social association in the singing schools as well as their common objection to the old lining-out of the Psalms, would tend to gather together in a group for the church services. Still, although there were organized and recognized choirs in the larger centers about 1750 (possibly earlier), the institution was not generally accepted by the more conservative smaller towns and country churches until during the 1760's and 1770's, and even later. Parish records show that gradual acceptance was often accompanied by the same sort of controversy that had characterized the first organized efforts to improve church music in the 1720's:

ROWLEY, MASSACHUSETTS—

1762. The parish voted, that those who had learned the art of singing may have liberty to sit in the front gallery. (They did not take the liberty.)

1785. The parish desire the singers, both male and female, to sit in the gallery, and will allow them to sing once, upon each Lord's day without reading by the Deacon.[25]

IPSWICH, MASSACHUSETTS—

As to seats for the choirs, they were designated by the First Parish in 1765, being "two back on each side of the front alley.". . . The choir of the First Parish began to sit in the gallery, 1781. This alteration was soon imitated in other parishes.[26]

WORCESTER, MASSACHUSETTS—

. . . in 1773, "the two hind body seats, on the men's side, on the lower floor of the meeting house" were assigned to those who sat together and conducted singing on the Lord's Day.

The final blow was struck to the old system by the resolution of the town, Aug. 5, 1779. "Voted, That the singers sit in the front seats in the front gallery. . . . Voted, That said singers be requested to take said seats and carry on the singing in public worship. Voted, That the mode of singing in

25. Parish Records of the First Church in Rowley, quoted in Thomas Gage, *History of Rowley*, p. 93.

26. Joseph B. Felt, *History of Ipswich*, pp. 212–13.

the congregation here, be without reading the psalms line by line to be sung."

The sabbath succeeding the adoption of these votes, after the hymn had been read by the minister, the aged and venerable Deacon Chamberlain, unwilling to desert the custom of his fathers, rose, and read the first line according to the usual practice. The singers, prepared to carry the alteration into effect, proceeded, without pausing at the conclusion: the white-haired officer of the church, with the full power of his voice, read on, until the louder notes of the collected body overpowered the attempt to resist the progress of improvement, and the deacon, deeply mortified at the triumph of musical reformation, seized his art, and retired from the meeting-house, in tears. His conduct was censured by the church, and he was, for a time, deprived of its communion, for absenting himself from the public services of the Sabbath.[27]

With the acceptance of the choir, a select group of trained singers who would naturally be attracted by music a bit too ornate and too difficult for congregational performance, begins the actual history of the anthem in New England.

But, before continuing with the account of the activities in the Colonies, it is necessary, for the purpose of establishing more objective standards for judging the efforts of the American composers, to digress briefly for a survey of church music in England during the late seventeenth and eighteenth centuries.

27. William Lincoln, *History of Worcester*, pp. 178–79.

II

Church Music in England
from the Restoration to
the American Revolution

W HEN THE STUART FAMILY was restored to the throne
of England in the person of Charles II on May 29, 1690, it
was, in a literal sense, the occasion of the restoration of decorative and artistic music to church services as well.

The Puritans had been in power for eleven years. During that time the
few organs spared by the iconoclastic destruction of the Civil War had been
silenced, the choirs disbanded, and church music throughout the realm had
been limited to unaccompanied, unisonal singing of metrical psalms.

After these years of relative austerity under the Puritan regime, it was
natural that a reaction should occur. The musical glories of the Elizabethan
and Jacobean ages were still fresh in memory, particularly so since John
Barnard published, in 1641, his *First Book of Selected Church Music*, a
monumental collection of services and anthems by the best English composers of the "Golden Age"—Byrd, Tye, Tallis, Gibbons, Weelkes, and others.
Consequently, upon the restoration of the monarchy and the old way of life,
there began in England a period of remarkable vitality in church musical
activity, an enthusiasm typical of all new cultures. And it was a new culture;
instead of gathering up the threads broken during the wars of 1642–46,
Charles II was to weave a new fabric designed after the French taste
acquired during his exile.

18

It is impossible to relate in one unified narrative the story of English church music during the late seventeenth and eighteenth centuries. So closely is the story involved in the political history and, particularly, the church history of the nation that the natural dichotomy between the Established Church and the dissenting groups is inevitably reflected in the musical developments as well. The music of the official Church of England is much more interesting, extensive, and important, of course. This main stream of church music will be considered first.

MUSIC IN THE CHURCH OF ENGLAND

The ban on decorative church music during the Commonwealth could hardly have been completely effective. It is probable that devout Anglicans among the aristocracy continued observance of the traditional liturgy with whatever musical resources were available in their private chapels.

The fact that William Child was permitted, in 1656 under the Commonwealth, to publish a new edition of his *Choice Psalms* (1639), with the title *Choice Musick to the Psalms of David for Three Voices, with a Continuall Base either for the Organ or Theorbo,* is in itself evidence not only that the letter of the law was sometimes evaded, but that there was a demand for that type of music. The reference to organs in the title is also significant. In the following year Oxford professor John Wilson, an ardent Royalist, published *Psalterium Carolinum. The Devotions of his Sacred Majesty in his solitudes and sufferings, rendered into verse set for three Voices, and an Organ or Theorbo* without jeopardizing his official position.

Certainly the interest in and desire for decorative music in the church service had not been destroyed by the official interdict, for the resumption of such activity was almost dramatically immediate. On the third Sunday after Charles's entry into London, June 12, 1660, Pepys recorded in his diary, "This day the organs did begin to play at White Hall before the King." [1]

Some of the older generation of composers who had been prominent in church music before the imposition of Puritanical restrictions were still living—Matthew Locke, John Wilson, Christopher Gibbons (son of the more illustrious Orlando), Benjamin Rogers, William Child, and Edward Lowe, to name a few.

Although the music of these older composers reflected the new Baroque techniques and ideals—expressive declamation, dramatic contrast—which had been gradually assimilated in England during the first half of the

---

1. Samuel Pepys, *Diary,* ed. Henry B. Wheatley, I, 164.

seventeenth century, they were too thoroughly imbued with the older English tradition of massive polyphony, dignity, and restraint to appeal to the new sovereign. Thomas Tudway, one of the first choristers in the Chapel Royal after the Restoration, recorded:

> The standard of Church Musick begun by Mr. Tallis, Mr. Byrd, *etc.*, was continued for some years after ye Restauration, and all Composers conformed themselves to ye Pattern which was set by them. His Majesty, who was a brisk and airy Prince, coming to ye Crown in ye flow'r and vigour of his Age, was soon, if I may so say, tyred with ye grave and solemn way, and ordered ye Composers of his Chappell to add Symphonies, *etc.*, with Instruments to their Anthems, and thereupon established a select number of his Private Musick to play ye Symphonies and Ritornellos which he had appointed. The King did not intend by this innovation to alter anything of the established way. He only appointed this to be done when he came himself to ye Chappell, which was only upon Sundays, on ye Mornings of ye Great Festivals and Days of Offerings. The old Masters, viz., Dr. Child, Dr. C. Gibbons and Mr. Lowe, organists to his Majesty, hardly knew how to comport themselves with these new-fangled ways, but proceeded in their Compositions according to ye old Stile, and therefore there are only some full services and anthems of theirs to be found. . . .[2]

In his history of English music, Ernest Walker accuses Charles II of setting up an authoritative standard of church music—a music characterized by an absence of "subjective religiousness," by cheerfulness, lively prettiness, attractive melodies, prominent rhythms derived from the current dance music, and emphasis on instrumental interludes; "declamation and general preference of solo to choral work were essential and sharply differentiating elements of the new order."[3]

To provide the new music for his chapel at Whitehall, Charles II called upon Dr. Child, Christopher Gibbons, Matthew Locke, Henry Lawes, Edward Lowe, and Captain Henry Cooke. Captain Cooke is frequently referred to in contemporary and later discussions of the music of the period partly because of the romance attached to his adventures as a Royalist soldier during the Civil War. But of much greater significance was Cooke's appoint-

---

2. Thomas Tudway, *Epistle Dedicatory to Lord Harley*. Tudway, a professof of music at Cambridge who had been a chorister in the Chapel Royal at the Restoration, was commissioned by Edward, Lord Harley, to transcribe a collection of anthems representing the period from the Reformation to Queen Anne's reign. The six thick folio volumes, now among the Harleian MSS of the British Museum, are prefaced by a history of English church music, continued in each successive volume, in the form of a dedicatory epistle to Lord Harley.

3. Ernest Walker, *A History of Music in England*, p. 142.

ment as Master of the Children of the Chapel Royal, in which position he was responsible for finding and training choir boys for the chapel service. His difficulties were recorded by Matthew Locke:

> For about a year after the opening of his Majesty's Chappell the orderers of the music there were necessitated to supply the superior parts of their musick with cornets and mens' feigned voices, there being not one lad for all that time capable of singing his part readily.[4]

His eventual success was almost spectacular; most of the major English composers of the late seventeenth century—Pelham Humphrey, John Blow, William Turner, Michael Wise, Thomas Tudway, and the greatest of all, Henry Purcell—were at one time "Captain Cooke's Boys."

The vitality of the early Restoration activity is attested by numerous publications of church music, especially of anthems and services. James Clifford, for example, issued two editions of his *Divine Services and Anthems* in 1663 and 1664. The second edition of this monumental work names the composers and contains the words of 393 anthems "usually sung in his Majesty's Chappell and in all Collegiate Choirs of England and Ireland."

Since some duplicate settings are indicated (setting of the same text by more than one composer), the current repertory only four years after the advent of Charles II comprised more than 400 anthems. Even earlier, in 1662, S. Buckley had published the words to the anthems used in York Cathedral, and manuscript choir books written at Durham between 1664 and 1670 (now in the Cathedral Library and the British Museum) contain nearly 300 anthems.

The content of Clifford's collection is of particular interest, since it reveals what music was available at the time of the Restoration. The Elizabethans are well represented by the majority of the works included; in addition there are works by William Child, Henry Lawes, Henry Cooke, Thomas Tomkins, Christopher Gibbons, and Benjamin Rogers (all of whom had not been included in Barnard's collection of 1641 because they had been living at the time) and fifteen anthems by the youthful choristers Richard Smith, Pelham Humphrey, and John Blow. Although most of the anthems are of the traditional "full" variety, there is a larger percentage of the newer verse anthems than there had been in Barnard's collection. The significance of the numerical proportions of full and verse anthems is debatable, however, since it is impossible to ascertain which were performed more frequently.

There is little doubt that the verse anthems, with their larger resources of

4. Matthew Locke, *The Present Practice of Music Vindicated*, p. 19.

instruments and solo voices in addition to the full choir, were the more popular, since they represented the preference of the court. Charles II's ensemble of twenty-four instruments of the violin family (as distinguished from the previously popular viols), an imitation of Louis XIII's "Vingt-quatre violons du Roi," must have been an exciting innovation for the younger composers in his musical establishment, but Evelyn probably represents the reaction of most of the older generation in his diary entry of December 21, 1662:

> . . . instead of the ancient, grave, and solemn wind-musique accompanying the organ, was introduced a concert of twenty-four violins between every pause [of the anthems and service], after the French fantastical light way, better suiting a tavern, or playhouse, than a church. This was the first time of change, and now we no more heard the cornet which gave life to the organ; that instrument quite left off in which the English were so skillful.[5]

The use of this large body of instruments in the chapel was destined not to survive after Charles II's death in 1685, but the "symphonies" and "ritornellos" introduced in deference to his taste were destined to become an integral part of English church music. After the "Twenty-four violins" were disbanded, the instrumental sections—now somewhat shortened—were played by the organ.

> Symphonys, indeed, with Instruments in ye Chappell, were laid aside; But they continu'd to make their Anthems with all ye Flourish, of interludes and Retornellos, which are now perform'd by ye Organ.[6]

The alacrity with which organs were rebuilt in the cathedral and collegiate churches throughout England is another evidence of the strong reaction against Puritan austerity. The Westminster Abbey organ was completed in November, 1660, just six months after Charles's arrival, and before 1670 organs were sounding at, for example, Exeter, Peterborough, York, Wells, and Magdalen College, Oxford. The instruments "were like the older English organs, small and without pedals. Parish churches remained organless; . . . not until the Oxford movement of the nineteenth century was one usually seen in a village church."[7]

To insure the authenticity of the Continental style among his chapel ensemble, Charles II even sent the most promising of Captain Cooke's choristers, Pelham Humphrey, to France and Italy to observe and study,

5. John Evelyn, *Diary*, ed. Austin Dobson, II, 199.
6. Tudway, *op. cit.*, fol. 3.
7. Henry Davey, *History of English Music*, p. 307. Pedals were added to the German Chapel organ in Savoy in 1772, and to the Westminster Abbey organ in 1792.

paying his expenses out of the Secret Service Fund! The investment was apparently fruitful, for, as Davey says, upon Humphrey's return from France, he

> inaugurated a style completely unlike the harmonic style of Tallis' *Dorian Service*, or the contrapuntal style of Orlando Gibbons' *Service in F*. Declamation was studied as carefully as in the Ayres and Dialogues of the period; but with a richer employment of purely musical resources. The anthem consisted of a series of short movements, some for solo voice, some choral. Though using more advanced and richer musical resources than their predecessors, the composers of the Restoration certainly did not attain a high ideal of sacred art; and the separate movements are too short and too slightly developed to be musically satisfying.[8]

Walker shares Davey's viewpoint when he typifies the Restoration anthem as consisting of "short disconnected movements, varied by instrumental sections of totally irrelevant character."[9]

The criticism of both these historians, although unduly harsh and unsympathetic, is understandable, coming as it does from men whose preference and standard are those of the polyphonic school of the late sixteenth century. But a different point of view and a rebuttal is furnished by Bumpus:

> The choruses in Purcell's verse anthems are generally short, but their brevity by no means diminishes their grandeur. The long-wrought oratorio chorus, however skillfully treated, cannot compare, in its grasp of interest on the hearer, with the few bars of chorus with which Purcell commonly winds up a verse anthem. In these choruses, however short, he invariably finds occasion for some surprising turn of harmony, or even a single note, that strikes a thunder clap.[10]

But, even if one concedes the weaknesses in the work of Humphrey and his colleagues, it is impossible to minimize the advantageous influence of his Continental indoctrination upon his pupil Henry Purcell, in whose music are combined the best resources of the traditional style and all the innovations of the seventeenth century—tempered, of course, by his artistic individuality.

In addition to the standard multisectional type so characteristic of the Restoration, another genre of anthem originated and flourished during the reigns of Charles II and James II (1685–88). This type is the cantata-anthem, so called because of its resemblance to the church cantata which was, at this same time, evolving on the Continent. It is a logical extension of the

8. Davey, *op. cit.*, p. 323.

9. Walker, *op. cit.*, p. 152.

10. John S. Bumpus, *A History of English Cathedral Music*, p. 159.

principle of sectional contrast seen in the multisectional anthems; but in these larger forms, instead of sections there are completely separated movements—some instrumental, some choral, some for solo voices or small groups of soloists.

The physical dimensions of these larger works usually limited their use to extra-liturgical occasions, although some were seemingly written for no purpose other than to exploit the available vocal and instrumental resources of a particular center of musical activity. After the turn of the eighteenth century, the cantata-anthem tradition was continued almost wholly in works for special occasions such as coronations, military victories, and royal birthdays. Handel's great Chandos anthems are exceptional in that they were written for and performed in the unique circumstances of the Duke of Chandos' private chapel. They were not intended for the general repertory of cathedral churches.

Historians of the period, both contemporary and modern, seem to be unanimous in concurring with Davey's pessimistic pronouncement:

> We have now reached the prosaic period [the eighteenth century] when England, for three hundred years distinguished by its musical skill, sank so far from its old repute as to acquire the name of an unmusical country. . . . Summing up the story of English music in the eighteenth century, it will be seen to be a fair type of the age—solid, prosaic, respectable and dull.[11]

If such a verdict were true, there would be a reasonable explanation for its application to church music, at least. For at precisely the same time to which Davey is referring, the Church of England "entered a period of feeble life and inaction: many church fabrics were neglected; daily services were discontinued; holy days were disregarded; Holy Communion was infrequent; the poor were little cared for; and though the church remained popular, the clergy were lazy and held in contempt."[12]

During the first half of the eighteenth century a new and promising generation of composers of anthems and services for the Church of England appeared, the most prominent being William Croft, Maurice Green, and William Boyce. Others of lesser musical stature and prominence were William Turner, John Weldon, Charles King, Thomas Kempton, James Kent, Thomas Kelway, William Hayes, and John Travers. Handel belongs to

11. Davey, op. cit., pp. 366, 431.

12. William Hunt, "Church of England," Encyclopaedia Britannica, 11th ed., IX, 469–70.

this generation, of course, but he does not figure in the main stream of English church music.

This lengthy list of notable church composers hardly supports Davey's verdict that England became an "unmusical nation" after the death of Purcell. Although, in comparison to the Continent, England produced relatively little music during the eighteenth century, it seems fairer to say that the prominence and popularity of the newer instrumental forms over the traditional vocal ones is largely responsible for the inordinate belittling of English efforts during the period. No new choral forms evolved during the period, so the vitality of the Continental developments in the new sonata and allied forms of instrumental music naturally claim the attention of historians and critics.

One has only to leaf through the pages of Croft's two-volume *Musica Sacra* (1724) or Boyce's three-volume *Harmonia Sacra* (1760–78) to realize that the eighteenth-century English composers of church music were inferior to those of the sixteenth and seventeenth centuries only in structural originality. They were content to follow the formal patterns of their ancestors, but their handling of musical materials was skillful and their presentation of the scriptural texts was effective. If there is a reduction in musical resources evident in their anthems and services, it is only a reflection of the general economy of means characteristic of the time on the Continent as well as in England. The works of these men are certainly completely adequate for the purposes for which they were intended and are expressive, valid works of art in an idiom congenial to their own generation, even though they are of smaller physical dimensions than the works with which they are often disparagingly compared (e.g., Handel's Chandos anthems).

The anthems of Purcell's successors continued to hover between allegiance to the older polyphonic ideals and the desire to meet the demands of a new taste. Sometimes an entire anthem was indistinguishable from one of the Elizabethan era; others sounded like operatic scenes with scriptural words substituted. But most were an amalgam of the two styles, with the newer dramatic idiom predominating.

With reference to the survival of the older English tradition mention should be made of the Academy of Ancient Music. This was a body of distinguished instrumentalists, both professional and amateur, formed about 1710 at the Crown and Anchor Tavern in the Strand. Their purpose was the study and performance of vocal and instrumental music, chiefly of the sixteenth and seventeenth centuries, but their more enduring contribution was the formation of a library of printed and manuscript music which preserved some treasures that would otherwise have been lost. Dr. Pepusch was a leader of the group until his death in 1752; their activities continued until the association was dissolved in 1792.

The next generation of English cathedral composers after Croft, Greene, and Weldon, and the last who might have served as a model for church music in the Colonies during the eighteenth century, must inevitably be represented by William Boyce. Lesser contemporaries were James Kent, William Hayes, and James Nares.

Even without taking into account the four volumes of his own excellent services and anthems, Boyce would deserve recognition as a major contributor to the history of English church music as a result of his publication, in 1760, 1768, and 1778, of three magnificent volumes entitled *Cathedral Music*, containing a selection of the best choral music representing composers from the time of Tye and Tallis down to John Weldon.

Credit for this monumental enterprise, the first collection of services and anthems printed in score in England, must be shared with Boyce's teacher, Maurice Greene, and with John Alcock of Lichfield Cathedral, both of whom had intended publication of such a collection. Dr. Alcock's proposal, as advertised in a small leaflet dated August 2, 1752, is reproduced here because of the revealing statement of the status of available music in the early part of the century:

> As the late famous Dr. *Croft* justly observes . . . (in the *Preface* to his *Anthems*) *That at this Day it is very difficult to find in the Cathedrals, any one ancient valuable Piece of Musick that does not abound with Faults and Imperfections; the unavoidable effect of their falling into the Hands of careless and unskilful Transcribers, which is an Injury much to be regretted by all who have any Concern or Value for those great Authors or their Works.* So it is likewise almost as difficult to find any modern *Service* or *Anthem* perfect, except perhaps just at that Church to which the Author belongs. . . .[13]

When Alcock heard of Boyce's intention, he graciously offered all the fruits of his preparatory labors. These materials, together with those bequeathed to his pupil by Dr. Greene in 1755, comprised the nucleus of Boyce's collection.

His own church music was published posthumously, the first volume in 1780 and the second in 1790. In 1846 a new edition by Vincent Novello added two more volumes of Boyce's works gathered from various sources.

From a stylistic point of view, Boyce represents his era admirably. The

13. Quoted in Bumpus, *op. cit.*, II, 257.

majority of his anthems are of the verse type, with emphasis upon the effective solo voice; yet these anthems manage to avoid any suggestion of the hedonistic. To his credit, also, is the fact that he escaped the indelible imprint of Handel, particularly creditable since this was the period which witnessed the genesis of the notorious English "Handel worship" as evidenced by the mammoth commemorative festivals held during the last half of the eighteenth century.

The English cathedral tradition was carried on late in the eighteenth and early nineteenth centuries by such composers as Benjamin Cooke and Dr. Samuel Arnold, but their works are of no concern to the present study. Not only was there little or no innovation, but these composers had no influence upon American church music before 1800.

There was, in addition to the major cathedral musicians, a class of English church composers who specialized in music designed for the smaller, especially rural, congregations of the Church of England. With meager musical resources, and a taste neither developed nor conditioned by the relatively extensive secular and instrumental music available in cities, these provincial congregations were attracted by decorative church music smaller in dimension and less pretentious in scope than that of the cathedral churches. Those who furnished this music were such composers as William Tans'ur, William Knapp, Joseph Stephenson, and John Arnold. They are rarely mentioned in histories of English church music because, between them and the major composers, there are so many lesser cathedral musicians who must be mentioned in the lists introduced by "other composers were . . ."

Very little is known about congregational music in the Church of England during the late seventeenth and early eighteenth centuries. This deficiency is understandable in view of the fact that those who recorded information about church musical affairs would naturally be attracted and primarily occupied by the more interesting decorative music of the anthems and by the activities of the cathedral composers.

Hymns, although popular with the dissenting groups, were not admitted by the more conservative Anglicans until the middle of the nineteenth century. Until that time congregational participation in music was confined to singing the old metrical versions of the Psalms and the chants. The most popular Psalters for those who read music were Playford's four-part setting of 1671, his three-part setting of 1677, and the collection of familiar tunes published with Brady and Tate's new version of the Psalms of 1696. These, and several other collections went through many editions during the following century.

According to Lightwood, "no matter what version might be in use, the tunes for the Psalms were common to all; and as the same tunes had been sung over and over again from generation to generation it is not surprising to find that singing in the Church of England services in those days [the early eighteenth century] was in a languishing state." [14] A few contemporary sources also furnish some insight into the state of congregational music. Unfortunately, the consistent nature of the evidence and of their criticisms makes the dreary picture that they paint a convincing one.

The Preface to John Playford's *The Whole Book of Psalms* (1677) implies that psalmody was not all that it should have been:

> But time and long use hath much abated the wonted reverence and esti-
> mation it had for about an hundred years after this establishment [the
> Reformation]: The Reasons whereof, as I conjecture, are chiefly these:
> 1. The faults that some find with the translation; 2. The dislike that others
> have for the Tunes; And 3. The ill custom of Reading every line by itself
> before they sing it. [15]

Such contention over church music is strikingly similar to the sort of arguments facing American churchmen at about the same time (see p. 7 ff. above). But more significant is the clear evidence that "lining-out" the Psalms was practiced in London as well as in country churches. Concerning that point, Playford continues later:

> Another reason, why singing of Psalms is very much obstructed in the
> true and right manner of singing, is the late intruding the Scotch manner
> of reading every line by the clerk before it is sung. . . . The two Prot-
> estant churches in London, to wit, the French and Dutch, I am
> sure have no such custom of reading the Psalms. I shall be willing to
> grant this way of reading to be useful in some villages near the sea, or in
> the Borders of Scotland, where it may chance not two in those Congrega-
> tions are book-learn'd; but not here in London, where in all Parishes, great
> or small, you have not three in a hundred but can read. [16]

The practice seems to have persisted to some degree in the Church of England throughout the eighteenth century. The Preface to Isaac Smith's *Collection of Psalm Tunes*, published about 1770, indicated that it was still common in English churches.

Thomas Mace, a contemporary of Playford, in his essay, *Musick's Monu-ment* (1676), directs most of his criticism toward rural parishes, lamenting that " 'Tis sad to hear what whining, toting, yelling, or screeking there is in

14. James T. Lightwood, *Hymn-Tunes and Their Story*, p. 121.
15. John Playford, *The Whole Book of Psalms*, Preface, p. [4].
16. *Ibid.*, p. [6].

many country congregations." His suggested remedy is an organ, but, recognizing the practical problem that the usual congregation could afford neither instrument nor organist, he offers a whimsical alternative:

> . . . I *will*, or any *Musick Master* will . . . *teach such a Parish Clark*, how to *pulse* or *strike most of our common Psalm Tunes*, usually sung in our *Churches*, for a *trifle*, (viz. 20, 30, or 40 *shillings;*) . . . and *then*, when *this Clark* is *thus well accomplished*, he will be so *doated* upon by all the *pretty ingenious Children*, and *Young men* in the *Parish*, that scarcely any of them, but will be begging now and then a *shilling* or *two* of their *Parents* to give the *Clark*, that he may *teach them* to *pulse a Psalm-Tune*. . . . And thus by *little* and *little*, the *Parish* in a short time will *swarm* or abound with *Organists* and sufficient enough for *that Service*.[17]

Describing the London scene of the next generation, Bumpus reveals that the church music had not improved much. In speaking of John Robinson, organist at Westminster Abbey during the 1720's and 1730's, he relates:

> As a harpsichord player Robinson was one of those nimble-fingered offenders who, in church, charmed their hearers with such music as was alone fit for that instrument. He introduced a practice calculated to display his digital agility in *Allegro* movements on the cornet, trumpet, sesquialtera, and other noisy organ stops, degrading the instrument, and instead of full and noble harmony with which it was designed to gratify the ear, tickling it with mere airs in two parts—in fact, solos for a flute and a bass, without any substratum of pedal passages. Parochial church music, as well, indeed, as the whole service, seems to have been sadly out of order at times during the portion of the century of which we are treating. The manners described by Addison and Steele in their "Tatlers" and "Spectators" certainly existed. There were jigs from the organloft, and vocal ladies in the congregation sometimes quavered and trilled an unreasonable time after the conclusion of the psalm.[18]

Davey also found that "the congregational psalmody of this period is not much alluded to, and we cannot form a very definite idea of it." He attributes to Magalotti a description of psalm-singing at Exeter, "first by one alone, then by all together." Without indicating the sources of his information, Davey continues:

> When there was an organ, the custom seems to have been to accompany the tune with a bass only; the florid figuration of the melody was still fashionable, and curious specimens of the style may be seen in Daniel

17. Thomas Mace, *Musick's Monument*, p. 11.
18. Bumpus, *op. cit.*, II, 212.

Purcell's "The Psalms set full." Both Churchmen and Dissenters practiced "lining-out;" where there was an organ florid interludes were played.[19]

The references to organs recall the circumstance that the instruments were extremely rare outside of large urban churches throughout the eighteenth century (see n. 7 above). A bass viol or a violoncello seems to have been the usual means of accompaniment for church music in those parishes where one was available. Toward the end of the century, other instruments of various kinds were admitted to double and support the voices. In the Preface to *The Compleat Psalmodist*, dated at Great Warley, Essex, July 19, 1779, John Arnold states:

> In this Edition, I have in the following Anthems and Psalm Tunes set the three upper Parts in the G Cliff, as I find it more eligible for country Choirs than the C Cliff; and since of late years several kinds of musical treble instruments have been introduced into many country churches, to accompany the Voices, as Violins, Hautboys, Clarinets, Vauxhumanes, etc., which Cliff is also more suitable to those instruments, and have placed the Tenor, which has the principal Air, and is designed for the leading Part, next the Bass, which also renders it much more convenient for Performers on the Organ.[20]

Congregational singing continued to be, as it still is, a matter of concern to those interested in high musical standards. In 1787, the Reverend W. Jones, vicar of Nayland in Suffolk, deplored that "the psalmody of our country churches is universally complained of as very much out of order, and wanting regulation in most parts of the Kingdom." [21]

MUSIC IN DISSENTING CHURCHES

The meager information available regarding the musical activities of Church of England congregations during the late seventeenth and eighteenth centuries is copious compared to the source material dealing with the dissenting groups [22] of the same period. This circumstance is particularly

---

19. Davey, *op. cit.*, p. 323.

20. John Arnold, *The Compleat Psalmodist*, p. iv.

21. Extract from a sermon quoted in Lightwood, *op. cit.*, p. 116.

22. Congregationalists (also known as Independents or Separatists) and Baptists formed the majority of the Dissenters. Presbyterians, Quakers, and Unitarians were smaller groups in England. The Puritans still considered themselves a reform movement within the Church of England, although they were looked upon as schismatics by the higher clergy and more orthodox communicants of that body.

unfortunate in terms of the present study, because an evaluation of American developments would be comprehensive only if they could be compared with those of an equivalent social and religious background in the mother country.

Church historians who have recorded the evolution of the growing opposition to the Established Church have practically nothing to say in regard to musical activities. Music historians, on the other hand, have been so absorbed with secular music that the little attention given to church music is devoted largely to the better-known anthem composers of the urban Anglican cathedrals. Even a specialized work on church music such as Bumpus' *Cathedral Music* has excluded by its titular limitations all but a nod of recognition to the "lesser" composers whose efforts were directed at the smaller sects.

This attitude, while regrettable, is justified to a certain extent. The composers of psalm tunes and anthems used by the dissenting bodies *were* "lesser" men, musically speaking. But it must be recorded in their defense that they did not have the technical training available to the choir boys in the larger centers, particularly in the Royal Chapel. Too, the musical taste of the predominantly rural membership of their churches did not demand an artistic standard comparable to that maintained in the cathedral churches. But it was, at least, equivalent to that of rural parishes of the Anglican communion.

In view of their influence not only upon the genesis of musical creation in the New World but upon a sizable segment of their own countrymen as well, however, it seems unjust that the most active and prominent representatives of their group should be unknown even to musical scholars; the names of Abraham Adams, Caleb Ashworth, Benjamin West, Aaron Williams, William Knapp, John Arnold, and William Tans'ur are vaguely associated with a few surviving psalm tunes—if they are remembered at all. Of those composers named, by the way, only Ashworth and Williams were members of Nonconformist denominations.

The inferior music of the dissenting groups can be excused partially on sociological and political grounds. These congregations were beset with troubles, both persecution from without and dissension from within, which did not hamper the Church of England.

Charles II, with a secret sympathy for the Roman Catholics, hoped to link their cause with that of the Puritans, thereby framing an effective opposition to the Anglicans. But, despite his policy of toleration and his precoronation promises of general amnesty and toleration to the Dissenters, he was not effective in curbing the excesses of a violently anti-Puritan Parliament. The

Act of Uniformity (1661), for example, drove all Puritan ministers (those not ordained by the Episcopacy) from their churches, and made Nonconformist worship punishable by fine, imprisonment, or, on third offense, transportation. After the Act of Uniformity there followed a quick succession of oppressive measures: the Corporation Act, the Conventicle Act, and the Five Mile Act of 1665, which forbade the ejected ministers even to visit within five miles of their former curacies. In an effort to stem this reactionary tide and to further his own interests (he had made a secret pact with Louis XIV for the conquest and partition of Holland and restoration of Roman Catholicism in England) Charles, with the support of his Cabal, issued the Declaration of Indulgence (1672) suspending the earlier oppressive measures. That he was not yet powerful enough to counteract Parliament became evident when he was forced to withdraw the Declaration and to sanction Parliament's Test Act (1673) requiring all public officeholders to be communicants of the Church of England. Eventually Charles himself was forced into an active persecution of Nonconformists as a reassurance to the Anglicans that he wholeheartedly supported their supremacy.

Persecution continued under Charles's successor, the Roman Catholic James II (1685–88), but with the accession of William of Orange in 1689 the period of overt oppression was ended. His Toleration Act (1689) granted freedom of worship to all Protestant groups except the Unitarians. With the exception of a comparatively few limitations (e.g., the Schism Act of 1714, which denied Dissenters the right of educating their own children) the period of external, or civil, impediments was ended, and the Protestants embarked upon an era of continuous development and expansion.

Unfortunately, there is no termination date for the internal troubles. Doctrinal disputes and controversies over matters of organization and procedure, combined with the geographic isolation of many rural congregations, continued to prevent unity of purpose and of action among the Protestants. Intra-congregational strife, often petty in nature, was particularly frequent during these early years. The ordering of, even the admissibility of, church music was frequently one of the grounds of contention.

During the days of the Stuart persecution, there was probably little music in the services of the dissenting groups because of the danger of detection. But with the toleration of William III and his successors the singing of metrical psalms flourished, if the extensive publication of Psalters and tune books during the late seventeenth and eighteenth centuries may be accepted as evidence.

While the quantity of church music waxed, the quality reflected the years of oppression. Lightwood speaks of "the utter indifference shown at this period [*ca.* 1700] to the singing of Psalms by the average congregation in the country churches. Very few possessed books; partly because they could not afford them, but more especially because they could not read." [23] To remedy this situation, a reform movement was inevitable:

> Early in the [eighteenth] century the Nonconformists began to turn their attention to the musical part of the services, and lectures on the subject were instituted at the old Weigh House Chapel in Eastcheap, one of the lecturers being the Rev. Dr. Grosvenor, pastor of Crosby Hall. The citizens of London were fond of instituting and supporting lectureships in those days, and these psalmody lectures were well attended. As, however, preaching without practising was of no use, a professor of psalmody was appointed to go round to the various meeting-houses and instruct the congregations in the art of singing.[24]

This view is particularly interesting since it is an exact parallel to the documented state of music in the churches of New England at the same time, even to the institution of singing schools. (See p. 15 above)

The music must have been somewhat limited if, as Davey maintains, the Protestants used no instruments. Although self-contradictory, Davey also tells of an interesting attempt to compensate for the lack of church organs as support for congregational singing. He describes an instrument called the "psalterer." Originating about the end of the seventeenth century, it was a large viol (resembling the tromba marina) with two strings, one for the melody and one for the bass line of psalm tunes. It seems unlikely that one performer would have been able to play the necessary double stops very effectively on an instrument of the dimensions suggested, but Davey claims that some psalm tunes were published in a tablature devised for the instrument and that a descriptive treatise was published. His tantalizing concluding phrase on the subject is to the effect that "nothing more is heard of the instrument although it might have been used advantageously where there was no church organ." [25]

Whether accompanied or not, in unison or harmonized, the music of those dissenting churches which admitted music at all (Quakers did not) seems to have been limited during the seventeenth century to psalmody alone. Early in the eighteenth century, however, the repertory began to be expanded by the acceptance of Isaac Watts's hymn collections, *Horae Lyricae* (1705) and *Hymns and Spiritual Songs* (1707).

23. Lightwood, *op. cit.*, p. 87.
24. *Ibid.*, pp. 112–13.
25. Davey, *op. cit.*, p. 329.

The introduction of non-biblical hymns, while quite revolutionary from a liturgical point of view, had hardly any musical significance. The familiar psalm tunes, some dating from Sternhold and Hopkins' collection, or new ones of exactly the same character served as the setting for the new religious poetry. What musical significance can be attributed to the introduction of hymns is purely circumstantial. The change in musical style of the congregational repertory that occurred during the eighteenth century would probably have occurred in the psalmody, but the fact remains that it was in connection with free religious poetry that there first appeared evidence of a new melodic floridity derived, obviously, from the anthems of Purcell and his contemporaries.

> Modern hymn-singing as we know it may be dated from the year 1740, when the earliest hymns of Charles Wesley—"the sweet singer of Methodism"—were collected and published under the title of *Hymns and Sacred Poems*. The next thing needed was a tune-book, and in 1742 appeared the first Methodist collection under the title of *A Collection of Tunes, set to Music, as they are commonly Sung at the Foundery*.[26]

The new style—no longer restricted to simple, syllabic settings of the text in long, even note values—is distinguished by the presence of two or more notes on one syllable, by greater incidence of triple meters in livelier tempos and by a heartier, more enthusiastic manner of performance for which the Methodists were famous. It is illustrated by the hymn tune "Resurrection" (still familiar today as the Easter hymn, "Christ the Lord is ris'n today"), which first appeared anonymously in the *Lyra Davidica*, a collection published in 1708.

The natural reaction of most Nonconformists was a conservative disapproval. The shifting of the balance between musical versus textual emphasis was a disturbing departure from a comfortable tradition inherited from more austere forefathers. But the vitality and success of the Methodist movement of the mid-eighteenth century, in which the new style played a prominent part, demonstrated the effectiveness of intrinsically attractive music as a catalyst to religious fervor.

From the 1760's on there appeared numerous tune collections for all denominations that included a large proportion of pieces in the new style; the Methodist revival alone accounted for some twenty or thirty collections.

26. Lightwood, *op. cit.*, pp. 121–22. "The Foundery" was an abandoned government foundry near Moorfields which had been wrecked by an explosion. Wesley bought it in 1739, and turned it into the first Methodist meetinghouse in London.

In addition to the tunes in the new style, these collections contained a type of congregational piece which was more novel still: the fuguing tune.

William Billings and his associates in New England have obviously been credited with too much originality in connection with this embryonic poly-phonic form. By implication, if not actual assertion, the fuguing tune has been closely identified with the American group without due recognition of the circumstance that they were simply imitating a model long popular in England.

Evidence of an even greater predominance of the aesthetic over the functional aspects of church music is also contained in these English tune books of the middle and late eighteenth century. In imitation of similar collections designed for Anglican congregations, the Protestant musicians began to include decorative pieces identified as "anthems" among the simpler psalm and hymn tunes.

An analytical description will be reserved for special treatment in the next chapter, because it was these anthems which served as models for the American composers with whom we are primarily concerned.

III

The Introduction of the Anthem into New England

THERE CAN BE LITTLE DOUBT that the infiltration of the anthem into New England during the 1760's and 1770's was a result of the singing-school movement which had originated about 1720 as an attempt to remedy the deplorable state of congregational psalmody. In the first place, these singing societies would have been the only agency furnishing a demand for that type of music; second, they were the only ones who *could* have sung it.

It is easy to reconstruct the probable sequence of developments leading to the acceptance of anthems into the worship service: having mastered the rudiments of singing by note, the singers became dissatisfied with the simple and familiar psalm tunes and welcomed the challenge of the more intricate anthems, a few of which were in almost every tune book. Then, after overcoming the technical difficulties, what would be more natural for the singers than that they should want to exhibit their achievements and share their exciting new experience with their parents and friends in the congregation?

The remarkable and revolutionary nature of the mere acceptance of the new decorative music into the worship service is apparent when one remembers that only a few decades earlier the controversy over the admissibility of singing psalm tunes by note was still lively. In some places separation of the better singers from the rest of the congregation was not yet allowed.

One would reasonably expect some evidence of opposition similar to the tracts and printed sermons of the 1720's and 1730's, but none seems to have survived, if any ever existed. There is not even an implication of opposition in the form of defense of anthems in the prefaces of the various tune books and collections where anthems first appeared. In view of the self-consciousness that attended other notable musical achievements by Americans during the eighteenth century (e.g., Hopkinson's claim that he was the first native American composer, or Billings' ill-concealed pride in his *New-England Psalm-Singer*), it is surprising that the appearance of anthems did not occasion any special recognition.

Actually, it is impossible to ascertain when and to what extent anthems first became regular and commonly accepted parts of New England church services Although their use by singing societies is extensively documented and their performance at special church services is occasionally mentioned, their acceptance into ordinary worship services during the eighteenth century must be assumed largely on the basis of their inclusion in the tune books designed for church use. And that assumption has a major weakness in that some of the collections make no reference to the church. Lowens is of the opinion that

> Such books as [Read's] *The American Singing Book* and *The Columbian Harmonist* were *not* designed for church use. . . . The use within the church of some of the music selected from the tune-books was quite incidental; the tune-books themselves were compiled to serve secular purposes.[1]

Although it is true that those particular collections by Read do not mention the church on their title pages, other collections of the same type do. The stated purpose of the books ranges all the way from *The Worcester Collection . . . for the Use of Schools and Singing Societies*, through an ambiguous reference to "Worshiping Assemblies" in the title of Stone and Wood's *Columbian Harmony*, to the unequivocal designation of Amos Bull's *The Responsary . . . adapted to the Use of the New England Churches*.

Leonard Ellinwood presents a more moderate version of the opinion that anthems were not used in ordinary church services.

1. Irving Lowens, Daniel Read's World. The Letters of an Early American Composer," *Notes* of the Music Library Association, ser. 2, IX (March, 1952), 245.

Within the confines of what is today the United States, church music throughout the seventeenth and much of the eighteenth century was limited to a few Psalm tunes or simple plainsongs. Although most of the tune-books contained a few anthems, there is little indication they were used to any extent in church services. Rather, they were employed more commonly as *pieces de résistance* in public concerts given by the singing schools and musical conventions. Only upon special occasions, in a few leading churches, were anthems performed during the eighteenth century.[2]

Ellinwood's conclusion is not unreasonable, but there is no more justification for drawing a negative inference from the lack of documentary evidence than for drawing a positive one. In his charming description of the choir in a small New England village at the turn of the nineteenth century, the Reverend Samuel Gilman noted that "a new anthem was gotten up at the recurrence of each Fast and Thanksgiving Day, and funeral anthems were sung on the Sabbath that immediately succeeded any interment in the parish."[3] If such industry was characteristic of a village choir, is it not probable that much more was accomplished in larger centers, particularly during or following an organized singing school?

The problem would be solved if some detailed contemporary descriptions of orders of worship followed in the eighteenth century had survived, but none has been located. This is probably another case where the commonplace nature of the information made a written record seem unnecessary to the participants. The only evidence encountered appears in a copy of Watts's *Psalms* (Boston, 1792) in the Houghton Library at Harvard University. In handwriting on the flyleaf of this volume is the following notation:

For the pulpit of the New North Society Meeting House.
Order of Service
The Singers commence with a short piece, without any Psalm being read.
1. Prayer
2. Reading the scripture
3. Singing
4. Sermon
5. Prayer
6. Singing
7. Blessing
Baptism is administered immediately before the long prayer.

The reference to "The Singers" as distinguished from simply "Singing" seems to indicate that a special group (the choir?) furnished the introduc-

2. Leonard Ellinwood, *The History of American Church Music*, p. 59.
3. Samuel Gilman, *Memoirs of a New England Village Choir*, p. 27.

tory music; items 3 and 6 probably referred to congregational psalmody. Whether the vocal prelude was an anthem or simply a tune sung by the choir alone cannot be determined. But, if it was an anthem, its prefatory function was obviously quite different from the position in the service and function as an offertory or "special number" that it acquired during the nineteenth century.

The first anthems known in New England were those found in English collections that had been imported for sale or brought over by new arrivals and travelers. It is impossible to determine how many of these collections existed in the New World and, consequently, the extent of their influence. But it is indisputable that among the models that guided the first American composers were these English anthems, for they were included regularly and frequently in American publications from the 1760's until well into the nineteenth century. The publications themselves indicate that there must have been some demand for this type of music. It is possible, but not very probable, that the pioneer publishers undertook publication without a reasonable assurance of financial profit, an assurance guaranteed by a preexistent market.

There seems to have been no discrimination on denominational grounds against any piece or collection of church music in either England or New England. Some of the composers were Anglicans, some Nonconformists. One of Aaron Williams' publications illustrates this catholicity in its title: *Psalmody in miniature . . . containing . . . all the tunes generally used in churches, chapels, or dissenting congregations.*

The first appearance of the designation "anthem" for a piece of music in an American publication occurred in a collection of tunes engraved, printed, and sold (and collected) by James A. Turner of Boston in 1752. This sixteen-page collection was obviously designed to be bound with the pocket-sized Psalters (about 14.5 × 9.1 centimeters) popular at the time; it is in that condition that the few surviving copies exist. In addition to a one-page instructional section headed "To learn to sing observe these rules," there are forty psalm tunes, one of which is entitled "Anthem to 100." The piece is a simple, three-part setting no different from any of the others and is of interest only because of the anomalous use of the word "anthem."

When the designation is next encountered, in 1764, it denotes the decorative type of music to which it was applied from that time on in the American publications of English anthems enumerated in the following survey.

To Josiah Flagg of Boston and Daniel Bayley of Newburyport must go the lion's share of the credit for introducing English anthems into New England. Flagg's biography is dishearteningly typical of many New

England musicians of the eighteenth century in that only a tantalizing fragment of his story has survived. Nothing is known about him before 1764 or after 1773 except an indirect reference in connection with a benefit concert in 1795 for a widow Flagg, mother of a "vile miscreant son," Josiah Flagg, Jr.[4] This villain might have been the junior of a different Josiah Flagg, of course. According to newspaper announcements, Flagg arranged at least five concerts for his own benefit between 1769 and 1773, when he notified the public that he was "about to leave the province soon."[5] The programs indicate that he was conversant with the best European music of the day (Handel is represented in all the concerts for which programs were printed in newspapers, Bach in one), a circumstance which suggests that he may have immigrated to the Colonies.

In 1764 Flagg published, in the oblong format copied from English collections and destined to become standard in America, *A Collection of the Best Psalm Tunes . . . to which are added some Hymns and Anthems, the greater part of them never before printed in America*. Included in the collection were two short, anonymous compositions designated as "anthems": "O praise the Lord" and "O give ye thanks unto the Lord."[6] These were either the first two, or two of the first three, anthems published in New England; in the same year, the sixth edition of Thomas Walter's *Grounds and Rules of Music* contained for the first time an anthem, William Knapp's "The beauty of Israel is slain."

Flagg's only other publication, issued in 1766, is much more significant in the evolution of the anthem in New England. It was the first sizable collection devoted primarily to anthems—there are a few psalm tunes— during the eighteenth century. Appearing either as *A collection of All Tans'ur's and a number of other Anthems from Williams, Knapp, Ashworth and Stephenson* or as *Sixteen Anthems, collected from Tans'ur, Williams, Knapp, Ashworth and Stephenson*, the compilation consisted of seventeen, eighteen, nineteen, or twenty anthems (contents varied in different printings) by the English composers named in the titles.

One year later, in 1767, appeared the first[7] American edition of William Tans'ur's *The Royal Melody Complete, or the New Harmony of Zion*, a popular English collection first published in London in 1755. The extent of

---

4. O. G. Sonneck, *Early Concert Life in America, 1731–1800*, p. 264.

5. *Boston Evening Post*, October 18, 1773, quoted in Sonneck, *op. cit.*, p. 264.

6. The latter is identified as a composition by William Tans'ur in one of Tans'ur's collections.

7. The first American edition is designated as the "third" on the title page in recognition of the two preceding English editions.

its influence in America is attested by no less than seven American editions between 1767 and 1774. The first edition seems to have been a corporate enterprise by W. M'Alpine of Boston, M. Williams of Salem, and Daniel Bayley of Newburyport, since all three are named as publishers on the title page; title pages for subsequent editions name only Bayley of Newburyport.

Daniel Bayley (*ca.* 1725–99) was the well-known organist of St. Paul's Episcopal Church in Newburyport, Massachusetts. The date and place of his birth and the details of his musical education are unknown. In Newburyport, where he resided from 1764 until his death on February 22, 1799, he conducted a printing and engraving establishment at his home opposite St. Paul's Church and kept a bookstore next door to the church. From there (and from Boston before his Newburyport press was set up in 1770) he issued eight eclectic collections, three of which, including the *Royal Melody Complete* mentioned above, contained anthems.[8]

With the "fifth" (i.e., third) American edition in 1769, the title of the Tans'ur collection was altered to *The American Harmony; or Royal Melody Complete,* and it was combined (and bound) with a modified version of Aaron Williams' *The Universal Psalmodist,* another popular English collection, which had been first published in London in 1763. The nine additional anthems in the Williams collection, added to the sixteen in Tans'ur's, produced a sizable source of repertory for the choirs and a valuable source of didactic models for the budding American composers.

Daniel Bayley continued to be the chief publisher of English anthems during the next decade, although the effects of the Revolution are apparent in the smaller number of new publications. In 1773 he compiled and published his *New Universal Harmony, or Compendium of Church Music* containing twenty anthems by seven English composers (see Bibliography under "Music") and, one year later, he published the largest single collection of anthems issued in the Colonies during the eighteenth century: *The Gentleman and Lady's Musical Companion* compiled by John Stickney (1744–1827), a farmer and teacher of singing schools from South Hadley, Massachusetts. Besides having more anthems than any other work, this monumental compilation was one of the largest (212 pages) of its kind published in America during the eighteenth century; it contained 30 anthems and 140 psalm and hymn tunes. Just what part Stickney played in the compilation is hard to determine. He was probably responsible for the choice

---

8. Frank J. Metcalf, *American Writers and Compilers of Sacred Music,* pp. 23–29. The "eclecticism" of some of the collections could be less politely termed "piracy."

and arrangement of the tunes, but Bayley certainly figured in the selection of the anthems. Not only are almost all the anthems from the Tans'ur-Williams collection included, but the same engraved plates seem to have been used for the new compilation. According to Evans, a new edition of Stickney's book appeared in 1783 in which "a considerable part of the old music is left out, and forty pages added, chiefly from *Harmonia Sacra* [an English collection], Law's, etc., with some new pieces never before published." [9] No copy of the revised edition seems to have survived.

The "Law's" referred to in Evans' quotation is either *Select Harmony* or *A Collection of the Best and Most Approved Tunes and Anthems*. Both were compiled by Andrew Law (1748–1821), a Congregational minister and music teacher of Cheshire, Connecticut, and were issued about the same time—late 1778 or 1779—by the publishing firm of Timothy and Samuel Green in New Haven, Connecticut. According to Evans, the *Select Harmony* appeared first in 1778, and other editions followed in 1779, 1784, 1786, 1792, and 1811; the other collection had only three editions, in 1779, [178?] and 1782. The few surviving copies of the two works, however, cannot be assigned unequivocally to positions corresponding to Evans' listing. For example, the two copies of *Select Harmony* in the Houghton Library at Harvard University, both lacking place and date of publication, are almost identical; the copy in the Boston Public Library is slightly different from both. The only extant copy identified as *A Collection of the Best and Most Approved Tunes and Anthems* (in the New York Public Library) lacks a title page. Since the contents of this book are almost identical with those of the three copies of *Select Harmony* inspected, either it is incorrectly identified as *A Collection of the Best . . . Tunes and Anthems* and is actually another edition of *Select Harmony* or it is an example of Law's publishing very similar works under different titles.

In either event, one (or both?) of these publications by Andrew Law shortly before 1780 contained thirteen anthems by English composers. It is worthy of note, also, that this was the first such publication outside of Massachusetts. This was the last relatively large collection of English anthems published in America, and its publication date suggests that Law might have had it ready before the three-year interruption of music-publishing activities during the war.

After the Revolution the growing sense of national consciousness in the new United States prompted a waxing enthusiasm for native products and a consequent waning of interest in and dependence upon English models.

9. Charles Evans, *American Bibliography*, item 18197.

English anthems did continue to appear in American publications through-out the remaining two decades of the century, but only as a few selected numbers among the American compositions and never in such large, unified collections as those of Flagg, Bayley, Stickney, and Law.

There were seven publications during the 1780's that contained English anthems, some new in America and some reprinted from the collections already described. The earliest was Simeon Jocelyn's *The Chorister's Companion*, published in New Haven in 1782 by the compiler and Amos Doolittle, an engraver who collaborated in the publication of several collections of church music. Jocelyn (1746–1823) was engaged in the publishing business in New Haven from 1782 until his death. Of the five editions of *The Chorister's Companion* listed in Evans,[10] only the first, the second (1788), and a Supplement (1792) are extant. The anthem contents of the two known editions vary considerably: the two English products (Thomas Everitt's "Great is the Lord" and a setting of the "Jubilate" by Tans'ur) in the first edition are omitted from the second and are replaced by five English anthems—two by Aaron Williams, one each by Tans'ur and Abraham Adams, and one by Clark and Green. The Supplement contains only psalm and hymn tunes.

In 1783 appeared the first of two editions of Oliver Brownson's *Select Harmony*, published in New Haven by the same Timothy and Samuel Green who had printed Andrew Law's collection of the same title four years earlier. A second edition was issued in 1791. The growing interest in American compositions is reflected in a pattern established by this work which was to be repeated in many later publications: an increasing proportion of American over English anthems in successive editions of the same work. Only one of the two English anthems, Knapp's "Is there not an appointed time," is retained in both editions. In the second, an anonymous[11] English "Oh that mine eyes would melt" is replaced by an American work.

Five English anthems were included in the next publication of the 1780's, *The Massachusetts Harmony, Being a Collection of Psalm Tunes, Fuges and Anthems . . . by a Lover of Harmony*. Published by John Norman in Boston, the collection has been occasionally attributed either to William Billings or to Andrew Law, but it is probably the work of neither, since Law was not in Massachusetts during the decade and Billings would not be likely to hide behind anonymity. Although no dates are given on the title pages of

---

10. Like many other publishers of his era, Jocelyn was not conscientious about precise identification of editions.

11. In Williams' *Royal Harmony* [*ca.* 1765] the anthem is attributed to "H: Purcel with a chorus by J: Clark." It has not been located among the known Purcell works.

either edition, Evans has assigned the first to 1784 and the second to the following year. The anthem contents, three by Aaron Williams and two by William Knapp, are the same in both editions.

In 1786, there appeared a large collection destined to be the most popular of its kind in New England during the remainder of the eighteenth century: *Laus Deo! The Worcester Collection of Sacred Harmony*. This handsome work was the first musical venture of one of the most influential American publishers of Revolutionary times, Isaiah Thomas (1749–1831), the founder of the American Antiquarian Society. Remembered primarily for his progressive newspaper, *The Massachusetts Spy* (published in Boston from 1770 until 1775, then in Worcester until well into the nineteenth century), and for his historical scholarship, Thomas must have had an above-average interest and education in music, for he seems to have been compiler as well as publisher of *The Worcester Collection*.

The work was divided into three parts: Part I, introductory instruction in the elements of music; Part II, about one hundred psalm and hymn tunes; Part III, many "Anthems, Fughes and Favorite Pieces of Musick." The first two parts were issued in eight different editions between 1786 and 1803, but they included no anthems until the sixth edition of 1797 when the newly engaged editor, Oliver Holden, inserted several American compositions. There seems to have been only one edition of Part III of *The Worcester Collection*, although a forthcoming revised version was announced in the Preface to the third edition of Parts I and II in 1791. The original form of Part III continued to be issued and bound with the successive editions of the other two parts, and the eleven English anthems (by Stephenson, West, Williams, Arnold, and Handel) were perpetuated in the repertory of the singing schools and choirs. Whether these anthems were significant as leaders or as followers of the public taste is debatable, although the latter circumstance would be more likely for the later editions at least.

In May, 1786, Amos Doolittle and Daniel Read of New Haven inaugurated an ambitious project in the publication of a monthly musical periodical entitled *The American Musical Magazine*. Read, a composer who will figure prominently in the chapter dealing with American composition, was probably responsible for selecting and editing the music. Doolittle (1754–1832) was the first engraver on copper in America and is best known for his engravings of the battles of Lexington and Concord. For some reason, probably financial, the scheme was abandoned in September, 1787, but not before twelve numbers had been issued, each consisting of four large (folio) pages containing secular songs, hymn tunes, and, occasionally, an anthem. During the year of publication, three English anthems were included:

Abraham Adams' "Be Thou my judge" in Number 5, Wanless' "Awake up, my glory" in Number 9, and Adams' "When the Lord turned again the captivity of Zion" in Number 11.

The last musical compilation by Daniel Bayley of Newburyport was issued in 1788. Entitled *The New Harmony of Zion,* the collection contained two English anthems: "Behold I bring you glad tidings" by Joseph Stephenson and "Tell ye the daughters of Jerusalem" by Clark and Green. Both anthems had appeared in earlier Bayley publications.

Sometime during the closing months of the 1780's *The Federal Harmony* was published by John Norman of Boston.[12] The popularity of this anonymous collection (erroneously attributed to Timothy Swan by Evans) is evident from the eight editions that appeared in the five years before 1794. Only the first two editions contained anthems by British composers; there were four in the first, three in the second. American products were featured in the remaining editions.

In American publications of the 1790's the inclusion of English anthems was more the exception than the rule. Only seven collections included such anthems during the decade, and only two of the seven had more than two. It is heartening to note, however, that most of the foreign compositions retained were the best of the English repertory available in America.

The first of these last-decade collections, Jacob French's *The Psalmodist's Companion,* was published by Isaiah Thomas of Worcester in 1793. The only non-American anthem included was an arrangement of "Already see the daughters of the Lord" from Handel's *Saul.*

In the same year, Thomas and his partner, Ebenezer Andrews, issued one of the largest and most popular American compilations of the half-century, Oliver Holden's two-volume *The Union Harmony.* The first volume, which went through three editions in 1793, 1796, and 1801, contained no English anthems. The second volume, "containing a large and valuable collection of Anthems, Odes, and Psalm and Hymn Tunes," included nine English compositions by Aaron Williams and Joseph Stephenson among its twenty-five decorative pieces. The original edition of Volume II seems to have been reissued with the revised versions of Volume I.

Holden's next collection, *The Massachusetts Compiler* (Thomas and Andrews, 1795), contained only one importation, Handel's "Let the bright Seraphim" from *Samson.*

12. Although no date of publication appears on the imprint, there is a reference to the publisher's office "near Oliver's Dock." Imprints from 1790 on, including the second edition of *The Federal Harmony* (1790), give Norman's address as 75 Newbury Street; so the first edition was probably in 1789.

the seventeenth century.[14] That may have been true of secular and instrumental publications, but the instructional introductions to most collections of church music still assigned specific tempi to the various metric signatures. The explanation of the "Moods of Time" in William Tans'ur's *American Harmony; or Royal Melody Complete,* being typical, is given here as a guide to the proper interpretation of the anthems of the period:

> The first Mood or Mark for *Common Time,* is a simple C, and denotes a slow grave Movement. The Crotchets in this Mood are to be sung in the Time of Seconds; so that 60 Crotchets, 30 Minims, or 15 Semibreves, are to be sung in the time of a Minute. The second Mood, which has a Line drawn across the Middle of the C, denotes a brisk Movement; the Time is to be beat and sung about half as fast again as in the Slow Mood: and when the C, is inverted, or turned backwards, or marked with a large Figure of 2, it denotes a very quick Movement, and is to be beat or sung about as quick again as the slowest Mood. . . .
>
> *Triple Time* contains 3 Minims, 3 Crotchets or 3 Quavers, in a Bar. . . . Three Minims in a Bar are marked thus 3/2 and are to be sung near as quick as Crotchets in slow Common Time. Three Crotchets in a bar are marked thus 3/4, and are to be sung about as quick as Crotchets in brisk Common Time, or the *Largo Mood.*[15]

Translated into modern metronomic speeds, the "moods of time"[16] are as indicated on page 49.

The meter is either duple or triple, and is most commonly one of the slower "moods." Syncopation appears frequently (especially the ♩ ♩ sarabande rhythm in triple meter) and tends to diminish the accentual effect of a metric scheme "tyrannized" by the bar lines.

The one really distinctive rhythmic feature is the apparent fondness for dotted patterns. Otherwise, the rhythmic patterns are simple and flexible, often dictated by the placement of strong and weak syllables of the text. Note values normally range through five degrees, from ♩ to ♪ but, except for the dotted patterns, most adjacent notes are either of the same duration or differ by only one degree (e.g., a quarter-note will be followed by a half-note, an eighth-note, or another quarter-note).

A lyric, cantabile melody is a prominent factor of the total musical effect at any given moment. When the whole choir is singing, the melody is

14. Curt Sachs, *Rhythm and Tempo,* p. 271.

15. William Tans'ur, *The American Harmony; or Royal Melody Complete,* 7th ed., pp. [7] and [8].

16. Tempos ascribed to those "moods" not described by Tans'ur are those assigned by Oliver Holden in *The Union Harmony,* 1793.

NAME AND SIGNATURE	TEMPO

COMMON TIME

First mood ("Adagio"), C	♩ = M.M. 60
Second mood ("Largo"), ₵	♩ = M.M. 90
Third mood ("Allegro"), Ɔ, Ɖ, or 2	♩ = M.M. 120
Fourth mood ("2 from 4"), 2/4	♩ = M.M. 160

TRIPLE TIME

First mood ("3 to 2"), 3/2	♩ = M.M. 60
Second mood ("3 from 4"), 3/4	♩ = M.M. 90
Third mood ("3 from 8"), 3/8	♪ = M.M. 120

COMPOUND TIME

First mood ("6 to 4"), 6/4	♩. = M.M. 60
Second mood ("6 from 8"), 6/8	♩. = M.M. 90

assigned to the tenor voice as was the practice in congregational psalmody and hymnody during the period. In the "verse" or solo sections, however, any of the four parts may sing the melody.

The ranges of the different parts are not very demanding of the singers. The composers seem not to have realized the possibilities of coloristic choral effects inherent in utilizing the entire natural ranges of the voices or in contrasting high and low tessitura. The bass part, in its harmonic function, regularly has the widest range, about an eleventh or a twelfth. The tenor melody covers a ninth or a tenth, and the women's parts, acting primarily as

treatment with an occasional melisma on some particularly appealing or descriptive word such as "rejoice," "glory," or "storm." There is also an occasional madrigalism such as a rising melodic line on "ascend" or "God is gone up," for example. Normal accentuation of the words of the text is generally preserved; yet it is paradoxical that although the musical material is seemingly motivated and determined primarily by the text, an inordinate amount of violence is done to the text (e.g., improper accentuation and the modification described above) because of purely musical considerations.

The foregoing description is a composite based on seventy-two anthems representing approximately twenty English composers and one Scandinavian published in New England between 1764 and 1800. The number of composers must remain an approximation because of several anonymous pieces which may or may not have been composed by the same person. In their dual function as useful repertory for the singers and as didactic models for American composers, the contributions of each of these composers, in chronological order of their period of greatest popularity in New England, will be surveyed in the following pages.

WILLIAM TANS'UR

If frequency of publication in New England were the only criterion, William Tans'ur, with his fifteen anthems appearing one hundred and twenty-eight times, would be indisputably the one English composer who exerted the greatest influence upon the American anthem composers of the late eighteenth century. Fortunately, quantity was not the determining factor.

What little is known about the man, his life and activities, is derived from his numerous publications of church music. Particularly interesting would be the derivation of the unusual spelling of his last name, for he was baptized "William Tanzer" according to the parish records of Dunchurch, Warwickshire. Further complication is provided by his gravestone and the parish register at St. Neots, Huntingdonshire, where his name is recorded as "William Le Tansur." [17] About 1730, according to Lightwood,

> he settled at Ewell, near Epsom, where he issued his *Melody of the Heart* [Preface dated 1735]. His first published work was *A Compleat Melody; or, The Harmony of Sion* [1734], which he himself stated to be "the most curiousest Book that ever was published.". . . William LeTans'ur, as he

17. I am indebted to the Reverend Canon L. Galley of St. Neots for this information.

afterwards called himself, was of a roving disposition, as he dates his books from various English towns. After teaching music and psalmody in various places he settled down at St. Neots, where he died in 1783. Credit is due him for having done his best to improve the condition of psalm-singing in the Anglican Church.[18]

The "various places" where he taught are identified in Brown and Stratton's dictionary as "Barnes (Surrey), Cambridge, Stamford, Boston, Leicester, and other parts of England." [19]

That Tans'ur's religious or pedagogical zeal was somewhat greater than his technique of composition was soon recognized by the New England singers. This is evident from his comparatively brief period of popularity: all except two of the one hundred and twenty-eight instances of publication in New England occurred during the decade immediately preceding the Revolution, 1764–74. The two anthems which survived the war years appeared in 1783 and 1788. The impression of immense popularity created by these figures is modified by the realization that Tans'ur's anthems appeared in only five different collections, one of which went through seven editions between 1767 and 1774.

For the sake of easier reference, the fifteen anthems [20] by Tans'ur which were printed in New England are given in alphabetical order in Table 1.[21] Following the list of anthems is a chronological listing of the publications in which the anthems appeared.

It is particularly appropriate that "O clap your hands" should be the last of Tans'ur's anthems that appeared in a New England publication. Not only was it one of the earliest published in this country (1766) and one of the two most popular, but it embodies most of the stylistic features that characterize Tans'ur and distinguish him from the other English composers. As his typical and representative work, it is reproduced in the Musical Supplement at the end of this volume.

The text is the Prayer Book version of Psalm 47, verses 1, 2, 5 and 6. Tans'ur frequently handled a Scriptural text with a great deal more freedom, but the nature of the license is revealed in a comparison of the two forms: (Tans'ur's modifications are in italics.)

18. James T. Lightwood, *Hymn-Tunes and Their Story*, pp. 110–11.

19. James D. Brown and Stephen S. Stratton, *British Musical Biography*, p. 404.

20. Tans'ur's "Praise the Lord" is indexed as an anthem in *The Royal Melody Complete*, but is not included in the present study because of its simplicity (in three parts, note-against-note style throughout) and brevity.

21. All anthems in this study are identified by the first line of the text. In the published collections they usually bore such titles as "An Anthem taken out of the 16th Psalm."

The only distinctive feature of Tans'ur's melodic style is the ornamental pattern which appears in measure 32 of "O clap your hands." This figure appears so regularly (in seven of the fifteen anthems) that it may be considered a Tans'ur "fingerprint," although some of the other composers use it occasionally. In all other aspects, the melodic style conforms to the general characteristics of the period described above.

It is in the element of harmony that Tans'ur's technical deficiencies are most readily apparent. Although the root-position triad is the basis of the harmonic scheme of all of the composers under consideration, it is with Tans'ur almost his only harmonic resource. For example, there are only nine inversions in "O clap your hands." The high proportion of incomplete triads, especially at strong cadential points, also contributes to the "primitive" quality—a quality, by the way, which has regained sufficient appeal that to modern hearers it may seem more an asset than a defect.

The harmonic progressions in "O clap your hands" are generally more orthodox than is usual in anthems by Tans'ur, although several characteristic weak progressions are present (e.g., in mm. 8–9, 11–12). The progression I-IV_6-V, which, with its alternate form I-VI-V, is another Tans'ur cliché, is illustrated in measures 19, 29, and 31. The absence of another of Tans'ur's common harmonic faults may account for the popularity of "O clap your hands"; such unjustified dissonances as those contained in the following passage from "They that go down to the sea" reflect either disregard for or ignorance of the accepted harmonic conventions of his day.

from: Flagg, Sixteen Anthems, 1766, p. 18.

FIG. 1. Tans'ur, "They that go down to the sea," mm. 16–19

Although there are occasional attempts at polyphonic writing in Tans'ur's anthems, his textural effects are usually limited to frequently varied combinations of the four parts and insertion of solo parts.[22] Such is the case in "O

22. Whether these solo passages were sung by one voice or by the whole section is a matter of performance practice that is not explained in the sources of the period. In the London editions of Tans'ur's *The Royal Melody Complete*, some of the single lines are marked "solo," others "tutt." These directions, except for an occasional designation "solus," were omitted from the American editions.

clap your hands." This frequent change of texture is partly responsible for the accusation of "fragmentation" sometimes used as evidence of the inferiority of eighteenth-century anthems. On the contrary, such textural variety might as reasonably be recognized as a virtue.

Typical of the composer's fondness of "madrigalisms" is the ascending melodic line at the words "God is gone up" in measures 15–17 of "O clap your hands." More imaginative is the angular depiction of the "drunken man" in the following passage from "They that go down to the sea":

from: Flagg, Sixteen Anthems, 1766, p. 18.

Fig. 2. Tans'ur, "They that go down to the sea," mm. 36–40

WILLIAM KNAPP

Ranking second to Tans'ur in number of anthems published in New England was William Knapp, the composer of the well-known hymn tune "Wareham." The ubiquitous nature of Tans'ur's primacy before the war is revealed in the comparison of Knapp's eleven anthems which appeared in only twenty-five publications before 1775 and Tans'ur's fifteen anthems which appeared one hundred and twenty-eight times. Like Tans'ur, Knapp was most influential in the pre-Revolutionary years, but it can be seen in Table 2 that his popularity continued to a greater extent (nine instances of publication in five collections) than that of Tans'ur after the war, although both disappeared from American publications at approximately the same time.

Even less is known of Knapp's activities than of Tans'ur's. He was born in 1698 or 1699 on the southern coast of England near Poole, Dorsetshire, where he resided all his life as a prosperous glover. He served as parish clerk of St. James's Church, Poole, for almost forty years before his death in 1768.[23] His two published collections, *A Sett of New Psalms and Anthems* (eight London editions between 1738 and 1770) and *New Church Melody* (five London editions between 1753 and 1764), have served as a means of identifying several of his anthems that appeared anonymously in New

---

23. I am indebted to Mr. Leonard J. Shaw, Borough Librarian, and the staff of the Public Library of Poole for information relating to Knapp taken from their newspaper archives.

Knapp's technical superiority is most evident in the elements of harmony, texture, and metric and melodic organization. Although the harmonic scheme is typically very simple, being based upon triads and progressions involving the primary chords, there are notably fewer instances of open fifths and of the unjustified dissonances so characteristic of Tans'ur. The cadences are usually upon complete tonic triads preceded by the dominant or dominant-seventh chord. There are instances of the V-I (incomplete) cadence, but such occasional use of that archaic device is not inconsistent with the common practice of the better-known composers of his day (cf. Mozart's *Requiem*).

from: Bayley, <u>New Universal Harmony</u>, 1773, p. 77.

Fig. 3. Knapp, "Hear O heavens," mm. 89–94

Like Tans'ur, Knapp's chief means of achieving musical variety is by textural contrast. But where Tans'ur was somewhat limited to a homophonic style by his lack of understanding of the mysteries of contrapuntal technique, Knapp is able to introduce confident passages of skillful imitation to relieve the monotony of a syllabic-chordal style. The superiority of Knapp's technique is only relative, however. His points of imitation soon dissolve into homophony after the final entry of the subject, but they acquire the dimensions of real fughettas when compared to Tans'ur's rudimentary attempts at imitative writing. The passage beginning at measure 20 in "The beauty of Israel" illustrates a duet style of polyphony frequently employed by Knapp. Another favorite textural device, obviously derived from Handel, is the sustaining of one part while the others move, as in Figure 3.

One further textural device should be pointed out in view of its later appearance in the works of American composers. That is the peculiar hybrid, which might be termed "textual polyphony," where the different parts are singing different words in the manner of polyphony while the lack of melodic and rhythmic interest in the different lines produces a basically chordal style. A passage from Knapp's "Bring unto the Lord" is an example (Fig. 4).

Another resource utilized by Knapp, in common with other composers and in contrast to Tans'ur, to achieve variety is that of meter. He usually alternates between duple and triple meter several times during the progress of an anthem. Since these metric changes almost invariably correspond with sectional divisions, they become formal elements as well. Missing, too, in Knapp's work are the awkward rhythms and misplaced accentuations of

from: Flagg, Sixteen Anthems, 1766, p.67.

Fig. 4. Knapp, "Bring unto the Lord," mm. 130–34.

Tans'ur, although the result is hardly a dancelike rigidity. Closely allied to Knapp's natural musical accentuations is his care in producing normal word accents, one of the most notable Tans'ur deficiencies. Not only is more respect shown the individual word, but there is much less license taken in modifying the Scriptural text by omissions and additions.

The qualities that distinguish Knapp's melodic style from that of Tans'ur are negligible but may be recognized as the product of more symmetrical contours and of a more integrated organization through sequences and motivic repetition. Where Tans'ur's melodic phrases often wander rather aimlessly around a keynote with no apparent consideration for contour, Knapp's have a more purposeful arrangement in the common melodic patterns of ascent-descent, descent-ascent, or simple movement either up or down. These features, plus the more economical use of figurate decoration, are illustrated in the passages from "I will sing unto the Lord" reproduced in Figure 5. Also worthy of note in Figure 5 are the extended harmonic (as

from: Bayley, <u>New Universal Harmony</u>, 1773, p.62.

Fig. 6. Williams, "O praise the Lord," mm. 29–46

1731, he was for a time a music engraver at West Smithfield, then clerk of the Scotch Church in London Wall, London. He died in London in 1776. Of his four known collections of church music, *The Universal Psalmodist* (London, 1763), *Harmonia Coelestis* (London, n.d.), *Psalmody in Miniature* (London, 1778), and *Royal Harmony* (London, *ca.* 1765), the first was particularly popular and appeared in numerous editions in England and America.

"I was glad when they said unto me," the most typical of Williams' anthems (see Musical Supplement), reveals that his style adheres closely to that found to be most typical of all English composers of the era (see pp. 47–52 above). Clearly superior to Tans'ur's, the style is very similar to that of Knapp. So close is the similarity, in fact, that it is difficult to understand why Williams continued to flourish in America after the Revolution while Knapp disappeared quickly from the repertory.

The minor differences between the two tend to identify Williams as being more inclined toward greater expressiveness. For example, the tempo fluctuations and the fermata in the closing section of "I was glad when they said unto me," the rests in the third section (mm. 75–87), and the unusually decorative final cadence introduce a dramatic quality lacking or minimized in the works of his contemporaries.

On the other hand, the high incidence of harmonic crudities (e.g., m. 103 of "I was glad . . .") and awkward harmonic progressions (e.g., mm. 20–21, 35–36) tends to negate the advantages of the more direct expressiveness.

An example (Fig. 6), though not really typical in the sense that the devices present are frequently employed, is included here as an illustration of the occasional evidence of Williams' more ingenious polyphonic technique. Strict canon between the treble and bass parts is maintained for nine measures at the beginning of the *Gloria*. Also striking is the instrumental character of the triadic point of imitation beginning in measure 40. As in "I was glad when they said unto me," the cadence is more ornate than is usual in Williams' anthems.

JOSEPH STEPHENSON

Joseph Stephenson's period of American publication corresponds almost exactly to that of Williams, although his appearances in New England collections were numerically fewer both before and after the Revolution. Six of his anthems appeared thirty-two times in the collections listed in Table 4.

The only known facts about Stephenson's life are told or implied by a marble slab over the pulpit in the Unitarian Church at Poole, Dorsetshire, an Independent meetinghouse built in 1704:

> To the memory of Joseph Stephenson, who for forty-five years, during which he filled the office of clerk of this meeting, manifested a steady attachment to the cause of religious liberty, the right of private judgment, and the practice of rational religion. His frailties—for frailties he had—(and

from: Law, Select Harmony, 1778, p. 94.

Fig. 7. Stephenson, "Sing, O ye heavens," mm. 179–88

CALEB ASHWORTH

Eight additional English composers whose influence must be assigned primarily to the pre-Revolutionary decade were of comparatively negligible importance. All except one are represented in New England publications by only one anthem, some by only one appearance of the single work.

"By the rivers of Babylon," by Caleb Ashworth appeared in five collections: Flagg, *Sixteen Anthems* (1766); Bayley, *New Universal Harmony* (1773); Stickney, *Gentleman and Lady's Musical Companion* (1774); and the two collections of Andrew Law of 1778 and 1779 (see p. 42). Born in 1722 at Clough-Fold, Rossendale, Lancashire, Ashworth was a student in Northampton of Dr. Doddridge, the hymn-writer, and spent his life as a Baptist minister and headmaster of a school in Daventry, where he died in 1775.[25] His only musical publication was *A Collection of Tunes*[26] which appeared in many editions after it was first issued in 1760.

"By the rivers of Babylon," taken from his published collection, shows Ashworth to be a skillful musical craftsman, though somewhat more reserved in expressiveness than Williams and Stephenson. There are no solo parts (the sections occasionally sing alone), and the only evidence of attention to choral color is limited to two duet-style antiphonal passages. One unique feature is the exchange of parts between treble and tenor in the written-out repetition of the final section. The momentary pre-eminence of the treble part is prophetic of the role it was destined to assume early in the nineteenth century.

The derivation of a setting of "Tell ye the daughters of Jerusalem" has been impossible to trace. It is identified only as the work of "Clark and Green" in Williams' *American Harmony, or Universal Psalmodist,* the source for Stickney's *Gentleman and Lady's Musical Companion* (1774) and the three postwar collections in which it appeared: *Worcester Collection, Part III* (1786); Jocelyn's *Chorister's Companion* (2d ed., 1788); and Bayley's *New Harmony of Zion* (1788).

First impulse prompts one to attribute it to Jeremiah Clark and Maurice Greene, two organists of the Chapel Royal in the early eighteenth century whose works were widely known and published in major collections of cathedral music. If this were true, they would be the only two of the more celebrated English church composers represented in American publications. Unfortunately, the musical idiom of the anthem strongly suggests that the composers were of the same breed of parish clerks and singing teachers encountered so far.

25. Biographical information from Brown and Stratton, *op. cit.,* p. 17, and Lightwood, *op. cit.,* p. 150.

26. A helpful guide to performance practice appears in the Preface to Part II of the collection: "*Verse* and *Chorus* chiefly refer to the organ, but the alteration denoted by them may be expressed by the voice: the former should be sung with a soft and low voice, or by a few of the sweetest voices; the chorus by all, with a bold tone and accent, and generally somewhat quicker than the other parts of the tune."

1753 as a clerk of Trinity Church. Establishing himself as an organist, choirmaster, and performer, he became one of the most active promoters of musical activities in that city during the three decades before his death in 1781. His successful effort to develop choirs and choral singing warrants special recognition, as does his direction of the first performance in America of Handel's *Messiah* in 1770—two years before its first performance in Germany.

Of the four anthems known to have been composed by Tuckey, only one, "Jehovah reigns, let all the earth rejoice," figures in the history of that form in New England, and that one has a peculiar history of publication. After its first appearance in Stickney's *Gentleman and Lady's Musical Companion* (1774), it was seemingly forgotten until 1799 when a revival in Benjamin's *Harmonia Coelestis* inaugurated its period of greatest popularity in the early nineteenth century. During this same time, however, the work seems to have been a favorite of Pennsylvania singers. It was performed on May 4, 1786, at a "Grand Concert of Sacred Music for the benefit of the Pennsylvania Hospital, Philadelphia Dispensary, and the Poor" and again at the first concert of the new Uranian Society in Philadelphia on April 12, 1787.[29] As early as 1805 (in Andrew Law's *Musical Magazine*, No. 1) the anthem had acquired the tune designation "Liverpool," and may be an instance of evolution through familiarity from the status of "special music" to that of congregational song.

The most immediately striking feature of the piece is the prominence of the rhythmic element resulting from the numerous "Scotch snap" patterns in the first section (see Fig. 10). Particularly interesting is the combination of that dotted pattern with evenly moving eighth-notes in measure 11. Not only is the combination of voices unusual (two trebles, tenor, and bass rather than the usual treble, counter, tenor, and bass), but the focusing of the melodic interest in the upper parts rather than in the tenor is quite progressive and prophetic. Other than the triadic nature of many melodic passages (e.g., m. 7), a genuine modulation to E-flat, the strict canon at the unison between the two treble parts (mm. 1–4), and the relatively large number of coloristic and semidramatic effects (mm. 5, 9), the work adheres closely to those characteristics of style found to be generally typical of the English product of the era.

The composers of three anthems published in New England before the Revolution have not been identified. The first was a short, simple setting of Psalm 117, "O praise the Lord," which appeared in Josiah Flagg's *A*

29. *Pennsylvania Packet*, May 1, 1786, and April 9, 1787.

from: Stickney, Gentleman and Lady's Musical Companion, 1774, pp. 189–190.

Fig. 10. Tuckey, "Jehovah reigns, let all the earth rejoice," mm. 1–12

Collection of . . . Psalm Tunes . . . and Anthems (1764). Since the work does not appear elsewhere, the only clue to the composer's identity is that he was an Englishman; all known composers represented in Flagg's collections were English. The anthem is essentially a duet for tenor and bass, with a perfunctory four-measure "Hallelujah" for chorus appended. Several harmonic dissonances and the string of five successive parallel fifths in

soon became particularly fond, so that in a few years almost every Country Church had one belonging to it; which in some places had the Distinction of the *Choir of Singers*, in others the *Society of Singers*; and, in very remote Places where they were not quite so polite, they had the Appellation of *the Singers* only, being, for the most Part, placed in a Gallery or Singing Pew, erected for that Purpose; and, in several churches, at the Expence of the Singers, by whom, in some Churches, not only the Psalms, but some very good anthems were performed in four Parts, by Persons with good voices and tolerable Skill; but within these few Years past, in many Places, the Singers, being fond of Novelties, are almost continually searching after all Publications of this Kind, when, perhaps, at the same Time, they have not learned half those Tunes they are already possessed of; but most of the Tunes which are now published, being Productions chiefly of Country Singing Masters, whose compositions (as the late Bishop *Gibson* justly observed) "Are as ridiculous as they are new"; and plainly prove that such composers are not acquainted with that Species of Music, which is proper for Parochial Singing, as their tunes mostly consist of what they call Fuges, or (more properly) Imitations; and are, indeed, fit to be sung by those only who made them; being not composed in the Style of Church Music, nor even founded on the Principles of Harmony, are therefore very improper to be introduced into the Service of the Church. . . .

Three of Arnold's anthems appeared in American publications, the first being "I beheld and lo a great multitude" in Bayley's *New Universal Harmony* of 1773. The other two, "The beauty of Israel" and "O sing unto the Lord," appeared in both the collections by Andrew Law in 1778 and 1779 (see p. 42), and the former was also included in the first edition of *The Worcester Collection* in 1786—a total of six instances of publication for the three anthems.

It is impossible to ascertain, in the sources available, how accurately these three anthems represent Arnold's style. But, even in view of the necessarily small sample that they constitute, a wide diversity of style, particularly in textural effects, is exhibited. There is such a wide diversity, in fact, that the suspicion arises that they are either the work of more than one composer or, at least, they represent very different phases in the development of one composer. There is reasonable basis for the former supposition. Composers of the "thirty-five capital anthems" in the earlier editions of *The Compleat Psalmodist* are not identified, and the implication of the title page is that they are by Arnold; in later editions, however, some of the same anthems are attributed to composers other than Arnold. For example, "Great is the Lord" (see p. 79) is erroneously attributed to Michael Wise in the seventh edition (1779) after appearing anonymously in the second edition of 1750.

One distinctive stylistic feature, evident in "O sing unto the Lord" (see Fig. 12), is a peculiar combination of conservative and progressive traits in Arnold's metric-rhythmic scheme. Although one meter is kept throughout the piece except for the closing "Hallelujah" (the other two anthems have no metric changes), great flexibility results from numerous syncopations and from successive appearances of a motif each beginning on different beats of the measure so that the triple pulsation is minimized rather than confirmed.

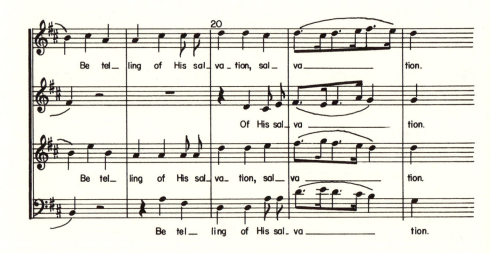

Arnold: "O Sing Unto the Lord"

from: Law, Select Harmony, 1778, pp.42-43.

FIG. 12. Arnold, "O sing unto the Lord," mm. 1–21

In some cases, the movement of the parts actually produces a temporary duple rhythm within the framework of the notation in triple meter (e.g., mm. 9–12).

A similar paradox exists in Arnold's harmonic idiom, where numerous unjustified dissonances occur within a system of chord relationships free from any of the awkward, archaic progressions encountered in so many anthems by other English composers.

The most distinctive feature of "O sing unto the Lord," its basic polyphonic conception, is, unfortunately, not a consistent trait of Arnold. The other two anthems named above have, in fact, less contrapuntal material than is usually found in the typical English anthem of the period. But in "O sing unto the Lord" the first section (mm. 1–41) is comprised of four successive points of imitation with only one brief insertion (mm. 14–18) of familiar style (see Fig. 12). After the two middle sections introduce textural variety of homophony and a counter solo, polyphony—now in "duet style"—returns for the closing section.

Finally, Arnold's treatment of the text is somewhat reminiscent of Tans'ur's in that he never hesitates to sacrifice normal word accentuation for the sake of musical rhythms. He does not, however, take as many liberties with the Scriptural text (i.e., omission, addition, or substitution of words and phrases) as did his older compatriot.

THOMAS EVERITT

A setting of Psalm 48, "Great is the Lord," appeared in two American collections, Bayley's *New Universal Harmony* (1773) and Jocelyn's *Chorister's Companion, Part III* (1783). It was thought, on the basis of Bayley's identification "taken from Arnold," to have been by John Arnold until Michael Wise was named as the composer in the last edition (1779) of Arnold's *The Compleat Psalmodist*. An earlier source [30] reveals, however, that it is the work of one Thomas Everitt, about whom nothing is known.

The anthem in question reflects a very conservative attitude in that it is simply a four-part "full" anthem, with successive points of imitation sometimes separated by small sections of familiar style. As is the case in Arnold's "O sing unto the Lord," the interplay of the various parts minimizes the accentual effect of the triple meter (e.g., mm. 4–7 in Fig. 13).

Although the contrapuntal technique is adequate, there is a surprising tendency to treat one or two of the four parts as harmonic "filler." Such is the case in Figure 14 where the tenor and bass (mm. 37–40) sing in canonic imitation while the treble accompanies the tenor part with harmonic intervals.

Surprising, too, is the primitive character of the whole harmonic scheme. There are quite a few dissonant combinations which cannot be explained in

30. Michael Broome (ed.), *A Choice Collection of Twenty-four Psalm Tunes.*

from: Bayley, New Universal Harmony, 1773, p.36.

FIG. 13. Everitt, "Great is the Lord," mm. 1–7

terms of the usual non-harmonic tones, and many violations of the "rules," such as parallel fifths and octaves. At the same time, this particular anthem affords us one instance of a device very rare, if not unique, in the English repertory of the present study—the chord of the augmented sixth in measure 35.

from: Bayley, New Universal Harmony, 1773, p. 38.

FIG. 14. Everitt, "Great is the Lord," mm. 34–40

ABRAHAM ADAMS

The question encountered in the works of John Arnold regarding the established identity of the composer applies equally to the four anthems attributed to, or "taken from," Abraham Adams in American collections. All four are traceable to Adams' very popular English collection (twelve known editions), *The Psalmist's New Companion* (London, n.d.), where the composers are not named. It is doubtful that Adams composed all the music for his collection, but, lacking information to the contrary, one must assume that he might have done so.

The available sources of biographical information regarding Adams are contradictory. According to Brown and Stratton, he flourished at the beginning of the eighteenth century and was organist at the church of St. Mary-le-bone, London, in 1710.[31] Eitner places him at the turn of the nineteenth century, saying that he came from Shoreham in Kent and played at St. Mary-le-bone in *1810*.[32] The sixth edition of his collection, a copy of which is preserved in the British Museum, indicates that he lived in Shoreham, Kent, about 1760; so it is unlikely that he was active as a church organist in either 1710 or 1810.

Adams' four anthems published in New England appeared in the following order: "They that put their trust in the Lord" in Stickney's *Gentleman and Lady's Musical Companion* (1774); "Be Thou my judge, O Lord" in the *American Musical Magazine*, No. 5 (1786); "When the Lord turned again" in the *American Musical Magazine*, No. 11 (1787), and in Pilsbury's *United States Sacred Harmony* (1799); and "Preserve me, O God" in Jocelyn's *Chorister's Companion* (2d ed., 1788).

from: French, Harmony of Harmony, 1807, p. 118.

Fig. 15. Adams, "Preserve me, O God," mm. 58–63

The pieces are generally conservative in character. Except for the more sophisticated harmonic vocabulary and a more faithful and accurate rendering of the Psalm texts, the style is strongly reminiscent of Tans'ur. The one distinctive feature is the occasional use of chromatically altered chords such as the augmented triad followed by a major IV chord in measures 60–61 of Figure 15.

31. Brown and Stratton, *op. cit.*, p. 2.
32. Robert Eitner, *Biographisch-bibliographisches Quellen-Lexikon*, I, 40.

BENJAMIN WEST

In the three anthems of Benjamin West which appeared in New England during the 1770's and 1780's is found some of the most original and distinctive music encountered in the works of the English composers under consideration. West is identified in standard reference sources only as an organist of the eighteenth century who composed *Sacra Concerto, or the Voice of Melody, containing . . . forty-one psalm tunes and twelve anthems* (London, 1760; 2d ed., 1769). The "Advertisement" in Andrew Law's *Select Harmony* (1778) relates further that he was a resident of Northampton, England, in order to distinguish him from a composer of the same name who lived in Providence, Rhode Island.

from: Law, Select Harmony, 1778, p. 79.

FIG. 16. West, "O clap your hands," mm. 57–67

All three of the anthems—"If the Lord himself," "O clap your hands," and "O Lord, our Governour"—appeared in Law's two collections of 1778 and 1779. The first and last named were also included in the first edition of *The Worcester Collection* (1786).

The progressive tendency in West's metric-rhythmic materials is immediately apparent in the frequent changes of meter, usually three or four within the course of a piece. It seems logical that, since the composer is utilizing metric contrast for a musical effect, the different pulsations would be clearly delineated. Such is not the case. There is a notable metric flexibility resulting from rhythmic patterns which contradict normal accentuation and from ties across the bar lines. All these devices are illustrated in "O Lord, our Governour" (see Musical Supplement), but nowhere are they so conspicuous as in the passage from "O clap your hands" where the rhythms produce a passage in 5/4 meter followed by a phrase in triple meter, both within a time signature calling for quadruple accentuation of the basic pulsation (Fig. 16).

Quite apart from its effect upon the meter, the rhythmic element acquires a large measure of prominence and intrinsic interest as a result of the introduction of triplets and of rhythmic mixtures (e.g., 2 against 3, 3 against 4) such as those contained in measures 45–46 of "O Lord, our Governor."

The melodic style, too, contains several outstanding and distinguishing features. The reliance upon sequences as a basic constructive device is illustrated in Figure 16 as well as in several passages in "O Lord, our Governour" (e.g., mm. 84–85). In the same representative work are examples of West's typically long melodic lines, extremely florid melismas, and an occasional tendency toward disjunct, harmonically motivated melodic movement rather than the more usual conjunct progression (e.g., mm. 61–64).

Finally, although West's textural arrangement is not basically different from that of the other English composers, there are two extraordinary devices which reveal a vigorous imagination if not a skillful contrapuntal technique. First, in two passages (mm. 34–37 and 84–86) of "O Lord, our Governour," he essays imitation at the distance of only one beat. Both attempts come off very well except for some harmonic difficulties that might well be printers' errors. Second, in "O clap your hands" is a charming little fragment of programmatic writing where he depicts hand-clapping by means of the ancient technique of hocket (Fig. 17).

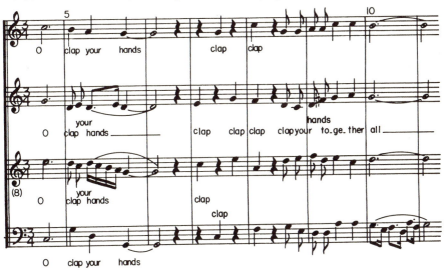

from: Law, Select Harmony, 1778, p. 78.

Fig. 17. West, "O clap your hands," mm. 4–11

A fourth anonymous English anthem, in addition to the three which appeared before the Revolution, was published in Oliver Brownson's *Select Harmony* in 1783. It is a setting of Psalm 44:1–4, "We have heard with our ears." Its title, "Anthem for America," in the Brownson collection is misleading in its suggestion of a patriotic motivation on the part of the composer, for it was found to have been taken from the London edition of Aaron Williams' *Royal Harmony*.

Lacking any other clue to the source, the musical style alone would reveal that it was not a native product. The technique of composition demonstrated is superior by far to that achieved by any American composer during the eighteenth century. The harmonic-tonal idiom is completely orthodox. Even more definitive of its origin is its formal conception; it is a wholly poly-phonic "full" anthem consisting of four dovetailed points of imitation. The opening measures, given in Figure 18, will suffice to illustrate the style of the whole anthem.

from: Brownson, Select Harmony, 1783, p. 73.

FIG. 18. "We have heard with our ears," mm. 1–20

WILLIAM SELBY

William Selby had a more direct influence upon New England's music than any of the other English composers, and, therefore, deserves a closer scrutiny. Like William Tuckey, he immigrated to the Colonies, but, significantly different from Tuckey, who lived in New York, Selby lived, worked, and composed in Boston in the midst of the activity with which this study is concerned. Because of that, he might be more properly included among the Americans in the following chapter, but since he received all his training in England and since he was a mature man and musician when he arrived in New England, and for the sake of consistency, he will be considered an English composer, leaving to the "American" category only those composers who were born in this country.

The earliest known fact about Selby's life is that he was organist at St. Sepulchre's Church, London, about 1767. His accompaniment of an anthem there in that year is recorded in Pohl's study of Haydn in London.[33] Nothing more is known about his life in England; even his birth date, 1739, must be deduced from his obituary notice in a Boston newspaper.

Soon after his arrival in Boston, in 1771 or 1772, he became organist at King's Chapel, a position he retained (except for a brief period as organist of Trinity Church, Newport, Rhode Island, in 1774) until his death in December, 1798. Numerous references to Selby in the Boston newspapers between 1772 and 1798 indicate that he was an energetic promoter of concerts, especially concerts of choral music. Such fruitful activity was the basis for an enthusiastic evaluation of the man and his contributions to the American scene by O. G. T. Sonneck. In Mr. Sonneck's opinion, Selby was the man

> to whom more than to Gottlieb Graupner or any other musician the glory is due of having indirectly laid the foundation for the Handel and Haydn Society, indeed the glory of having prepared the musical future of Boston more than any other musician before or after him. . . .
>
> Boston's musical history during the last thirty years of the eighteenth century may be said to have centered in the personality of this interesting and ambitious musician.[34]

The three anthems known to have been composed by Selby appeared in print at least twelve times before 1800. That comparatively high incidence of publication is a reflection of the popularity of the pieces.

33. C. F. Pohl, *Mozart und Haydn in London*, II, 212.
34. Sonneck, *op. cit.*, pp. 270, 287.

The earliest extant evidence of Selby's activity as an anthem composer is an announcement in the *Boston Gazette* of August 26, 1782, of the publication of two anthems, "one taken from the 100th Psalm for four voices (that was performed at the Stone Chapel on the 30th of April) the other taken from the 17th Psalm, for three voices, composed in an easy and familiar style, and adapted for the use of Singing Societies." [35]

The setting of Psalm 117, "O praise the Lord, all ye nations," seems not to have appealed to the singers and the public; it was not published elsewhere, and there is no reference to it in any of the programs described in the newspapers. If Selby insisted upon performance in the key in which it was written (D major), wherein the treble and tenor parts gravitate around high A's, the reluctance of the singers is understandable.

Psalm 100, "O be joyful in the Lord," was immensely popular. After the initial independent publication, it appeared at least five more times: in *The Federal Harmony*, unnumbered editions of 1790, 1792, 1793, and the eighth edition of 1794; and in Holden's *Union Harmony*, Vol. II (1793). The second recorded performance—though it undoubtedly was not the second, the piece having been in circulation since 1782—took place at a mammoth "Concert of *Sacred* Musick, vocal and instrumental, at the *Chapel Church*, on Tuesday, the 10th day of this present month of January [1786], for the benefit and relief of the poor prisoners confined to the jail of this town. . . ." [36] It was listed as the eleventh item on the program as "Then the *Jubilate Deo*, or, 'O be joyful in the Lord, all ye lands,' is to be sung, as and for an Anthem, by the voices accompanied by all the instruments."

The concert was such a phenomenal success, both financial and musical, that a correspondent of a Philadelphia newspaper was impelled to forward a lengthy critical review to the *Pennsylvania Herald*. The account mentions Selby's anthem: ". . . the doxology composed by Mr. Selby gave great satisfaction on Tuesday last at the Chapel church, and was only excelled by his anthem, in which he has not disgraced the inspired, royal author of the 100 psalm." [37]

A similar concert "for the benefit of those who have known better days" is recorded in the *Boston Gazette* of January 15, 1787. Again Selby's work is mentioned in a subsequent review where the correspondent records that "the Jubilate Deo, or C. Psalm, set to musick by Mr. Selby, gave

35. The "17th Psalm" was an error; it should have been the "117th Psalm."
36. *Massachusetts Gazette*, January 2, 1786.
37. *Pennsylvania Herald*, January 28, 1786, quoted in Sonneck, *op. cit.*, p. 277.

universal satisfaction, the choruses in which are worth of admiration." [38] In the same year, the anthem was included in a concert for the raising of funds to be used in rebuilding the meetinghouse in Hollis Street; and it was possibly one of the two unidentified "full Anthems composed by Mr. Selby" performed in connection with the festivities honoring George Washington upon his visit to Boston in the fall of 1789.[39]

The other unnamed "full anthem" may have been Selby's "Behold He is my salvation," which appeared with the notation "never before published" in *The Worcester Collection*, 1786; subsequently it was included in the 1790, 1792, and 1793 editions of *The Federal Harmony* and in Holden's

from: The Worcester Collection, 1786, p.162 and p.165.

Fig. 19. Selby, "Behold He is my salvation," mm. 110–14, 183–86

Union Harmony, 1793. Although it is not mentioned by name in any of the newspaper accounts of concerts, one performance is recorded in connection with its first publication: "By Mr. William Selby, Organist of the Chapel in Boston, New-England. Performed at the opening of the Old South Meeting House in said town."

"O be joyful in the Lord" (see Musical Supplement), the most popular of the three works, contains almost all the typical stylistic features of the other

38. *Boston Gazette*, January 22, 1787.
39. *Massachusetts Gazette*, October 14, 1789.

two. The missing details are such coloristic devices as the choral unison and the several "madrigalisms" (e.g., on "shout") illustrated in Figure 19.

In "O praise the Lord" there is a much greater proportion of imitative polyphonic writing than is present in the other two. No fewer than six points of imitation are introduced, all of which soon dissolve into chordal homophony, however. One piquant harmonic detail of the same piece is Selby's use, in three different passages, of a descending succession of triads in first inversion, a latter-day fauxbourdon.

Many of the stylistic features of "O be joyful in the Lord," as well as of the other two works, suggest that Selby's vocal music was more strongly influenced by instrumental music of the later eighteenth century than that of any other composer encountered so far. For example, his metric-rhythmic scheme plays a rather prominent role in the total musical effect, thanks largely to a strong accentual quality in the fast tempo suggestive of dance music. Here there is no metric obscurity; the rhythmic patterns, often a reiterated figure, emphasize the basic duple or triple pulsation, although occasional progressive devices such as superimposed triplets (e.g., mm. 66–67) introduce rhythmic variety.

Selby's melodic style also suggests an instrumental conception in the frequent triadic progression, the many sequential passages, and the generally short phrases. He was certainly not thinking in vocal terms when he wrote, in "O praise the Lord," a bass part demanding a range of over two octaves, from low D to middle E.

The harmonic, tonal, and textural materials all reflect a closer affinity to the instrumental idiom of the late eighteenth century than to the vocal style of the waning Baroque period common to most of the other English composers. Modal chord progressions, unjustified dissonances, and incomplete triads are very rare exceptions. "Textbook" progressions, with a particular emphasis on tonic, dominant, and subdominant triads, characterize the harmonic idiom, and produce clearly defined tonal centers. And these tonal centers are utilized as formal elements. In the *Jubilate Deo*, for example, the clear C major of the first and third sections is contrasted by unequivocal modulation (as distinguished from transitory excursions in the relative key) to A minor for the counter and bass duet in the middle section.

The prevailing texture is another echo of late eighteenth-century instrumental style. There is only one suggestion of polyphony (mm. 5–8) in "O be joyful in the Lord," and that is in a non-imitative duet style. To compensate for the vitality usually furnished by counterpoint, however, there is great variety in voice combinations and in special effects such as the antiphonal and responsorial exchanges in measures 23–36 and 110–15.

One other influence upon Selby is so obvious that it hardly needs to be pointed out. Substitute for the words "and His mercy is everlasting" in measures 75–87 the phrase "King of Kings, Hallelujah" and it becomes apparent that the ubiquitous shadow of G. F. Handel fell across the Atlantic Ocean as well as the English Channel.

George Frederick Handel

The fame and popularity of Handel in New England during the eighteenth century is not in the least adequately reflected by the extent to which his works appeared in American publications. Although numerous performances of his works (mostly selections from oratorios) are recorded in newspaper announcements and reviews of concerts from about 1770 on, only six of his works were printed only eight times before 1800. This seeming paradox has a twofold explanation: first, many of the performances were given, or organized, by English immigrants; and, second, English editions of the works were undoubtedly imported for use by choirs, singing schools, and musical societies.[40]

The choice of selections printed in New England and the curious transformations to which they were sometimes subjected furnish an interesting insight into the tastes of American publishers and the resources of American singers during the period. A recitative and chorus, "Already see the daughters" and "Welcome, mighty King" from *Saul*, was the only work by Handel printed in America before the Revolutionary War. It was included in Flagg's *Sixteen Anthems* (1766) as "A song in Mr. Handel's Oratorio of Saul." (Almost thirty years later, the same work appeared in Jacob French's *Psalmodist's Companion*.) The recitative was reproduced just as it appears in the Complete Edition except that it was marked for "Tenor Recit°." rather than for soprano. Several modifications were necessary in the chorus parts, however, to meet the limitations of local resources.

Handel's setting of "Welcome, mighty King" is for three women's voices with a figurate accompaniment by carillon (an instrument of the glockenspiel type played from a keyboard), violins, oboes, viola, and continuo. In the Flagg version, the instrumental parts are omitted completely, and the three voice parts are assigned as follows: soprano I to tenor, soprano II to treble, and contralto to bass. The two top parts are interchanged in order to conform to the American practice of giving the melody to the tenor voice. The only other differences in the Flagg version are the omission of a

40. The substance of this section on Handel appeared in the *Musical Quarterly*, April, 1959. It is included here by permission of G. Schirmer, Inc., the copyright owner.

repetition of the short phrase beginning with "ten thousand praises" and a slight reharmonization of the final cadence. The motivation for the latter alteration is an enigma—unless the editor *wanted* parallel fifths.

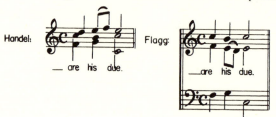

from: Flagg, 16 Anthems, 1766, p.9.

FIG. 20. Alternate cadence for Handel, "Welcome mighty King"

A puzzling hiatus of twenty years elapsed before Handel was again represented in a New England publication. Then, in 1786, the first edition of *The Worcester Collection* contained two works attributed to Handel, an anthem on Psalms 66 and 134 ("O praise the Lord with one consent") and the "Grand Hallelujah Chorus" from the *Messiah*.

The first-named is a simple, hymnlike setting in four parts ending with a five-part section at the words "O be joyful in God all ye lands." A search through the printed works of Handel has failed to reveal the source. It is possible that Mr. Thomas was mistaken in the composer's identity, but since the work does not appear elsewhere, there is no further clue. The opening phrase is reproduced here in the hope that some reader may be able to identify the source (Fig. 21).

from: Worcester Collection, 1786, p.166.

FIG. 21. Handel[?], "O praise the Lord," mm. 1–7

It was with ill-concealed pride that the editor included the "Hallelujah Chorus" with no modification except omission of the instrumental accompaniment. In a note addressed "To the Lovers of Psalmody in the New England States," he offered the following explanation:

> Having been favored with a copy of the Grand Chorus in that celebrated work, The MESSIAH, by Handel, one of the greatest musicians that ever delighted the ears of mortals, I am happy to give it a place in this collection. Although it has been thought by some, too hard to be learned, and too delicate to be sung, even by the best performers in this country, I doubt not but that there are many, who have not only skill to learn but judgement to perform it, at least equal to some of the best singers in Europe.[41]

Newspaper accounts of vocal concerts indicate that the singers were not so reluctant as the editor would have his readers believe. Considering that the selection had been publicly performed several times in New York, Boston, and elsewhere during the 1770's, it is indeed surprising that it had not been printed before 1786. Equally inexplicable is the fact that it did not appear again during the eighteenth century.

Almost a decade elapsed before two more Handel excerpts were printed in Daniel Read's *Columbian Harmonist, Number III* in 1795. They were "An Anthem on the Resurrection" ("Since by man came death" from the *Messiah*) and "A Christmas Anthem" beginning with "There were shepherds abiding in the fields" from the same oratorio. According to Evans the latter work was also published as an independent piece by Read in the previous year, 1794.[42]

Read's version of "Since by man came death" included only the vocal parts of the two solo quartets and two choruses printed on pages 268–71 of Volume 45 of the Handel *Gesamptausgabe*. No distinction is made between the solo and choral sections as was done in the original setting.

More liberties were taken with the recitative and chorus, "There were shepherds abiding in the fields" and "Glory to God," than with any of the other pieces. In fact, the setting of the recitative section is wholly original (by Read?). What motivated the arranger to presume to "improve" upon Handel's setting is a mystery. The beginning of the American version is given in Figure 22 because of its intrinsic interest and for purposes of comparison with the original.

As had been the case with the other choruses, the vocal parts of "Glory to God" were preserved intact, but instead of omitting the instrumental accompaniment altogether, it was here simply abridged and "arranged."

41. *Worcester Collection*, 1786, p. 106.
42. Evans, *op. cit.*, item 27087.

from: Read, Columbian Harmonist No.3, 1795, pp.9-13.

FIG. 22. Read(?) "There were shepherds abiding in the fields," mm. 1–21

While the voices are singing, the instruments double the vocal parts instead of furnishing an independent figuration. The extent of the modification is illustrated in Figure 23. It should be pointed out, too, that the very presence of "symphonies" in an anthem intended for American singers is a very rare exception.

from: Read, Columbian Harmonist, No.3, 1795, p. 12.

Fig. 23. Handel-Read, "Glory to God," mm. 1–10

In the *Massachusetts Compiler* (1795) occurred the last publication of a Handel selection in New England before 1800. The work hardly conforms to the "anthem" classification, since it is the aria "Let the bright seraphim" from *Samson*. Only two parts, the melody and the bass line, are reproduced in this collection. Here, again, "Symphony" is indicated for the introduction and interludes, but only the first violin and bass parts of the original orchestration appear.

Ample evidence of Handel's popularity in New England is furnished by newspaper accounts of programs if not by frequent publication of his music. Josiah Flagg, in whose collection of 1766 a Handel work first appeared in a local publication, seems to have been the first Handel enthusiast in Boston. Handel is represented on almost every concert arranged by Flagg beginning with the opening "Overture Ptolomy" at a concert in May, 1771.[43] The Handelian banner was passed on from Flagg to William Selby, who perpetuated the enthusiasm until the end of the century. The success of Selby's evangelism was reflected in an ecstatic review of his tremendous benefit concert of January 16, 1787:

> . . . The Song from the oratorio of Jonah, sung by Mr. Deverell, was beautifully affecting but *Handel! Handel! Handel!* The song from his oratorio of Sampson "Let the bright Cherubim, etc." sung by our townsman, Mr. Rea, could not be excelled by anything but the Hallelujah Chorus in the Messiah, in which there appears perfect illumination—the surprise and astonishment of the audience, at the performance of this divine Chorus, cannot well be described, especially at those parts where the *drums* so unexpectedly thundered in and joined in the glorious Hallelujahs to the "King of Kings and Lord of Lords. . . ."[44]

The extent to which Handel's influence was felt in New England is a proposition for the next chapter, but, whether or not they took advantage of it, it is gratifying that the finest possible model of choral composition was available to the American composers.

ROBERT ROGERSON

Dr. Robert Rogerson, like William Tuckey and William Selby, was an English immigrant to the Colonies. Unlike the other two, he followed music only as an avocation.

Born in Portsmouth, England, in 1722, he came to America sometime before 1750. On July 2 of that year he was installed as the second minister of the church at Rehoboth, Massachusetts, where he remained until his death in 1799.[45] He must have been an accomplished singer, for he was one of the soloists (in his sixty-ninth year) at a concert given in King's Chapel, Boston, on December 1, 1789. This was a concert, probably under the direction of William Selby, which was intended for performance before George Washington on his visit to Boston but which was postponed until after his departure.

Nothing is known about Rogerson's musical training in England and nothing regarding his musical activities in this country, except the concert mentioned above and his one publication, *An Anthem, Sacred to the Memory of . . . John Hancock, Esq.*, published in October, 1793. Beginning

---

43. *Boston Evening Post*, May 13, 1771.
44. *Boston Gazette*, January 22, 1787.
45. William Allen, *American Biographical Dictionary*, 3d ed., p. 712.

with the phrase "Know ye not that there is a great man fall'n this day?" the work reveals a competent musicianship and a progressive concern for emotional expressiveness, but it was not very influential in the development of the anthem in New England because it was an independent publication and because of its special nature as an occasional piece.

HANS GRAM

Hans Gram, the non-American composer whose anthems were the last to be introduced into New England during the eighteenth century, was an anomalous figure. All other foreign composers who served as models for Americans were Englishmen, albeit naturalized in the case of Handel.

Gram was a native of Denmark, "liberally educated at Stockholm," who settled in Boston sometime before 1790, and served as organist at the Brattle Street Church during the last decade of the century.[46] Nothing more is known about him except for his publications during that same period. Several of his instrumental and secular pieces appeared in Isaiah Thomas' monthly *Massachusetts Magazine* between 1789 and 1791. One of these has the distinction of being the first orchestral score printed in the United States, "The Death Song of an Indian Chief"—probably the first musical expression of American nationalism as well. For the occasion of the entombment of John Hancock, he published a short *Sonnet for the 14th of October, 1793.*

In the field of church music his major contribution was *The Massachusetts Compiler* (1795) of which he was a co-compiler with Oliver Holden and Samuel Holyoke. One of the notable features of that collection is an excellent introductory section, "Theoretical Observations," for which Gram was probably responsible. Admittedly derived from prominent European theorists (e.g., Fux, Rousseau, Avison, D'Alembert), it was far superior to, and much more extensive (34 pages) than, the rudimentary "Rules of Music" common to most tune books.

Gram's three known anthems were published in 1793 and 1794: "We'll sing to God with one accord" in his *Sacred Lines for Thanksgiving Day* (1793); "The first man was of the earth," published independently as *Resurrection: An Anthem for Easter Sunday* (1794); and "Praise ye the Lord"[47] in *The Worcester Collection* (5th ed., 1794).

His schooling in the Continental instrumental style of the late eight-

---

46. Metcalf, *op. cit.*, pp. 134–35.

47. The title is "An occasional Anthem, dedicated to the Singing Societies of Newburyport by their humble servant Hans Gram. Charlestown, October, 1794."

eenth century is clearly reflected in Gram's anthems. An instrumental accompaniment is required only in the last anthem, "Praise ye the Lord," but there is a strong suggestion of an instrumental idiom in the *concertino-ripieno* exchanges between treble and tenor duet and the full chorus in "We'll sing to God with one accord," and in the trumpet-call figures in "The first man was of the earth."

"Praise ye the Lord" is included in the Musical Supplement as a representative work even though it is a bit more pretentious than the other two. Its most striking features—the bass recitative with continuo accompaniment, the obviously instrumental character of the figuration in measures 60–62, and its setting for six-part mixed chorus—were unique in the literature available to New Englanders. The clear sectionalization, the triadic nature of much of the melodic progression, the fully developed harmonic idiom, the homophonic texture, and the great variety in choral color (e.g., choral unisons, mm. 4–6, 137–41) are consistent in all three works. The reason for Gram's one harmonic mannerism is puzzling: the third of the chord is missing from seventh chords in root position. That the omission is willful is unmistakable in the penultimate chord of "Praise ye the Lord," where there are six parts available for the four-note chord, but he chooses to adhere to his usual practice.

In one sense, Gram should be grouped with the New England anthem composers rather than with those who furnished models for the Americans. Unlike the Englishmen, he was not transplanting the fruits of a vast heritage of choral church music. His contribution was the application of a superior musical training (probably German in derivation), the idiom of Continental instrumental music, imaginative musicianship, and taste to a form that was probably as new to him as it was to the native New Englanders. In this sense it is ironic that Gram's anthems are more interesting than any others, English or American, published in New England during the eighteenth century. And his beneficial influence is directly traceable in the works of those with whom he was associated in church music and publishing activities—Oliver Holden, Jacob Kimball, Samuel Holyoke, and Isaac Lane.

IV

Anthems by

New England Composers

PUBLICATION OF ANTHEMS by native composers began in New England in 1769. Before the end of the century a treasury of approximately one hundred and twenty anthems by twenty-one composers had been made available to choirs and singing schools.

It would be gratifying, in the interests of the present study, if New Englanders had produced the very first anthems in the Colonies, but that distinction must go to Philadelphia and to those two unwitting contenders for the title "first American composer," Francis Hopkinson and James Lyon. And just as an unequivocal primacy of one or the other as the first American composer can never be established on the basis of known evidence, so it is impossible to ascertain which wrote the first anthem.

In the Library of Congress is a manuscript music book bearing the inscription "Francis Hopkinson His Book. Philadelphia, Domini 1759." On page 180 of that collection begins "An Anthem from the 114th Psalm" signed "F. H. 1760." (Two additional anthems are included that might have been written by Hopkinson, but both are anonymous.) Possibly referring to this anthem, the *Pennsylvania Gazette* of May 15, 1760, described the commencement exercises of the College of New Jersey, relating that "one of the Students who received his Master's Degree on this occasion, conducted the organ with that bold and masterly Hand for which he is celebrated and several of the Pieces were also of his composition." [1]

Since Hopkinson was among the candidates for the Master's degree on that occasion and since he was the only one famed for his musical accomplishments, Sonneck reasonably concludes that his compositions were performed.

It would seem that Hopkinson had been established as the first American anthem composer, but the next issue of the *Pennsylvania Gazette*, May 22, 1760, carried the following announcement:

> Proposals For Printing by Subscription. A Choice Collection of PSALM TUNES and ANTHEMS, from the best Authors, with some entirely New, and a number of Dr. Watts' and Mr. Addison's Hymns set to Music.
> To which will be prefixed the plainest and most useful rules of Psalmody. By James Lyon, A.B. [2]

Three months later, a notice regarding the same collection announced that "the Engraver and Printer have both begun to engrave and print the said tunes, and are determined to compleat them as soon as possible." [3]

The collection, Lyon's *Urania*, was not actually offered for public sale until 1762, but since the manuscript of the book must have been completed at the time of the second announcement, the two anthems by Lyon that appear in the collection were obviously composed during the early part of 1760 at the latest.

Thus the evidence stands; Hopkinson and Lyon must share the distinction of being the first American anthem composer. But Lyon assumes a greater significance in that his were the first *published* anthems, and, as such, could exert an influence upon the development of the form not only in Pennsylvania but in New England as well.

Lyon's music is germane to the history of the anthem in New England because of the fortuitous circumstance that the composer was available when the newly formed Presbyterian church of Machias, Maine, was looking for a resident minister in 1771 or 1772. Lyon went from Nova Scotia to Machias about that time as a result of financial difficulties and remained there until his death in 1794.

In addition to his presence in the area, one of the two anthems by Lyon in *Urania*, "Let the shrill trumpet's warlike voice," appeared in the 1769 and

1. Oscar Sonneck, *Hopkinson and Lyon*, p. 81.
2. *Ibid.*, p. 134.
3. *Pennsylvania Journal* (Philadelphia), July 24, 1760.

1771 editions of Aaron Williams' *American Harmony, or Universal Psalmodist* and in Stickney's *Gentleman and Lady's Musical Companion* of 1774. Because of its intrinsic interest as one of the first compositions by an American composer and as the first American anthem published in New England, it is included for convenient inspection as Figure 24. Despite its brevity and the many incomplete triads, it is a very attractive and competent setting of a metric version of the last Psalm with notable attention given to choral color (the three voices appear in all possible combinations), to independence of line, and to ornamental figuration in the soprano part.

A third edition of *Urania* was published in New York in 1773, and Sonneck speculates that another might have been issued, "perhaps in New England," after 1773. Even if the fourth did not exist, the third edition was certainly available for distribution in Maine by Lyon. It is unlikely that an edition was published in Maine; there is no known instance of music publication in that state before 1800.

Eighteenth-century anthem publication in New England was confined to Massachusetts, Connecticut, and New Hampshire, and was centered, naturally, in the larger cities. Boston was the most prolific, with fifty-four collections or single pieces (counting all editions); thirty-six were produced in New Haven. Other towns and villages where anthems were published, with the number of publications indicated in parentheses, were Newburyport, Massachusetts (16); Exeter, New Hampshire (11); Cheshire, Connecticut (9); Northampton, Massachusetts (5); Salem, Massachusetts (4); Worcester, Massachusetts (2); Wallingford, Connecticut (2); Simsbury, Connecticut (1); Hartford, Connecticut (1); Watertown, Connecticut (1); Dedham, Massachusetts (1); and Medway, Massachusetts (1). It is interesting, by the way, to note the remarkable self-sufficiency, as evidenced by local engravers and printers, of some of the smaller communities during the eighteenth century in comparison with modern industrial concentration.

Productivity in anthem composition in the various localities was reflected proportionately by the volume of publication. The first and most extensive activity was in Boston, where New England's first native anthem composer was its first known composer of any music, the magnificent William Billings.

Just as he dominated the whole scene of church music in New England during the last three decades of the eighteenth century, Billings towers far above the specialized group of anthem composers. Among the twenty-one men who comprise that special group, he alone furnished more than a third of all the anthems composed. His most prolific successor produced only twelve anthems compared to Billings' forty-seven.

An Anthem. Taken from Psalm 150th

J. Lyon

from: Williams, _American Harmony_, 1771, p. 60-1.

FIG. 24. Lyon, "Let the shrill trumpet's warlike voice"

WILLIAM BILLINGS

William Billings was born in Boston on October 7, 1746, was apprenticed to a tanner in his youth, became a teacher of psalmody—and, as such, the first American professional musician. He died in poverty on September 27, 1800, at the home of his eldest daughter.[4] Some biographers record that he became the proprietor of a music store in Boston, the scene of the famous episode of the two cats, but this conclusion seems to be based largely on a notation in the *Boston Evening Post* of November 5, 1764, to the effect that tickets for a forthcoming concert could be had at "Mr. Billings' shop near the Post Office." There is no indication of the type of shop or of which "Mr. Billings," but it seems unlikely that William, the tanner's apprentice, would have been the proprietor of his own shop at the age of eighteen. That the probate record after his death described him as a tanner and that the nickname, "The Musical Tanner," persisted throughout his lifetime seem to indicate that he continued in that trade in addition to his musical activities.

Billings was married to Lucy Swan, one of the singers in his music class in Stoughton, Massachusetts, on July 26, 1774. Nine children were born to the union; six survived infancy.

As for the character of the man, the effusive and picturesque introductions to his tune books, too frequently quoted in a patronizing context, are the most revealing sources. In addition, two valuable and reliable descriptions by contemporaries are extant. One particularly timely account appears in the diary of William Bentley, an editor and pastor in Salem, Massachusetts. It was written on Sunday, September 28, 1800, two days after Billings' death:

> William Billings, ae. 60, died in Boston. This self-taught man thirty years ago had the direction of all the music of our churches. His "Reuben" [*The Singing Master's Assistant*], as he whimsically called it, with all its great imperfections, had great fame and he may justly be considered as the father of our New England music. Many who have imitated have excelled him, but none of them had better original power. His late attempts, and without a proper education, were the true cause of his inferior excellence. He taught the singers at the Brattle Street Church in 1778 with great approbation, and his fame was great in the churches. He was a singular man, of moderate size, short of one leg, with one eye, without any address, and with an uncommon negligence of person. Still he spake and

---

4. Two major sources of biographical information regarding Billings are Frank Metcalf's *American Writers and Compilers of Sacred Music*, pp. 51–64, and Carl E. Lindstrom's, "William Billings and His Time," *Musical Quarterly*, XXV (October, 1939), 479–97.

sang and thought as a man above the common abilities. He died poor and neglected and perhaps did too much neglect himself.[5]

The other description is that by Billings' close friend, Dr. Pierce of Brookline, Massachusetts, as recounted to Nathaniel Gould and quoted in his *Church Music in America* (p. 46). Dr. Pierce and Governor Samuel Adams were fellow choirmembers of Billings for many years, and the three met together occasionally for recreational singing.

In addition to the evidence of his many publications and his widespread influence, two surviving documents attest to the fame and prestige that Billings enjoyed during his lifetime. In the Preface to *The Worcester Collection* of 1786, the compiler, as justification for the large proportion of American compositions included, said:

> Mr. William Billings, of Boston, was the first person we know of that attempted to compose church music in the New England States. His music met with approbation. Some tunes of his composing are inserted in this work. . . . Several adepts in music followed Mr. Billings' example, and the New England States can now boast of many authors of church music whose compositions do them honor.[6]

Finally, an obituary notice in the *Columbian Centinel* of September 27, 1800, noted: "Died. William Billings, age 60 [i.e., 53], the celebrated music composer. . . ."

All except one of Billings' forty-seven anthems first appeared in five of the six collections of church music published by the composer between 1770 and 1794 (see Table 5). The exception was an independent publication of "God is the King" issued about 1783.

The number of collections listed in Table 5 indicates to some extent Billings' popularity among singers in New England before 1800. The one hundred and one instances of publication represented are five times as many as his nearest rival could boast.

Publication of the anthems as special pieces inserted into collections that were primarily devoted to psalm and hymn tunes was not Billings' original intention. He had a much more ambitious design, which can be traced through the "Advertisements" of the first three collections to its frustrating, yet hopeful, dissolution.

In *The New-England Psalm-Singer* (1770) Billings indirectly appealed for the readers' approval by announcing: "If this work should meet with encouragement, it may be an inducement to the author to publish

---

5. Metcalf, *op. cit.*, p. 63.
6. *Worcester Collection*, p. [2].

TABLE 5

PUBLICATION IN NEW ENGLAND OF ANTHEMS BY WILLIAM BILLINGS

And I saw a mighty angel (6, 17, 22) *
As the hart panteth (1)
The beauty of Israel (6)
Behold how good and joyful (10)
Blessed is he that considereth the poor (1)
Blessed is he that considereth the poor [another setting] (6)
By the rivers of Watertown (2–5)
Down steers the base (6)
Except the Lord build (11)
God is the King (7)
Hark! Hear ye not (23)
Hear, O heavens (23)
Hear my prayer, O Lord, give ear (1)
Hear my prayer, O Lord, my God (2–5)
The heavens declare (23)
I am come into my garden (23)
I am the Rose of Sharon (2–5, 9, 16)
I charge ye, O ye daughters (23)
I heard a great voice from heaven (2–5, 12, 18, 22)
I love the Lord (2–5)
I will love Thee, O Lord (23)
Is any afflicted (2–5)
Let every mortal ear attend (6)
Lift up your eyes (10)
The Lord descended from above (1)
The Lord is King (1)
The Lord is ris'n (11, 13–15, 18–19, 21, 24, 25, 26–28, 29–30)
Mourn, Phar'oh and Ahab prevail (23)
My friends, I am going (23)
O clap your hands (11)
O God my heart is fixed (23)
O God, Thou hast been displeased (23)
O praise God (20, 23)
O praise the Lord of heaven (23)
O Thou to whom all creatures bow (23)
Samuel the Priest (10)
Sanctify a fast (23)
Sing praises to the Lord (23)
Sing ye merrily (2–5)
The States, O Lord (2–5)

They that go down to the sea (6, 16)
Thou, O God, art praised in Sion (6)
Vital spark of heavenly flame (6, 8, 9, 12, 16, 25)
Was not the day dark and gloomy (2–5)
We have heard with our ears (23)
When the Lord turned again the captivity of Zion (23)
Who is this that cometh (6)

Date	Publication	Number of Anthems
1. 1770	Billings, *New-England Psalm-Singer*	5
2. 1778	Billings, *Singing Master's Assistant*	9
3. 1779	The same, 2d ed.	9
4. 1781	The same, 3d ed.	9
5. n.d.	The same, 4th ed.	9
6. 1781	Billings, *Psalm-Singer's Amusement*	9
7. 1783	Billings, independent publication	1
8. 1783(?)	Jocelyn, *Chorister's Companion, Part III*	1
9. 1788	The same, 2d ed.	2
10. 1786	Billings, *Suffolk Harmony*	3
11. 1786	Billings. Bound with no. 10 but not paginated as part of that collection	3
12. 1786	Langdon, *Beauties of Psalmody*	2
13. 1792	*Federal Harmony*, 3d (?) ed.	1
14. 1793	The same, 4th (?) ed.	1
15. 1794	The same, 8th ed.†	1
16. 1793	Shumway, *American Harmony*	3
17. 1793	French, *Psalmodist's Companion*	1
18. 1793	Holden, *Union Harmony*	2
19. 1796	The same, 2d ed.	1
20. 1794(?)	Billings, independent publication	1
21. 1794	Read, *Columbian Harmonist, No. II*	1
22. 1795	The same, *No. III*	2
23. 1794	Billings, *Continental Harmony*	17
24. 1797	Mann, *Northampton Collection*	1
25. 1797	Brownson, *A New Collection*	2
26. 1794	*Worcester Collection*, 5th ed.	1
27. 1797	The same, 6th ed.	1
28. 1800	The same, 7th ed.	1
29. 1798	*Village Harmony*, 4th ed.	1
30. 1800	The same, 5th ed.	1

* See note to Table 1 for explanation of numbers in parentheses.
† Other editions not located.

another volume, which he has in possession, consisting chiefly of anthems, fuges, and choruses of his own composition." [7] Eight years later, having met with the sought-after encouragement, he offered explanation for the delay in the "Advertisement" to *The Singing Master's Assistant:*

> By way of apology, I take this method to acquaint the Public, that the Book of Anthems which I promised them was just upon the point of publication, When hostilities commenced between Britain and the Colonies; which Unhappy War was the sole motive, that induced me to "hang my harp upon the willows" and suppress the publication; but relying so far upon their Candour, as to suppose myself already forgiven, I here renew my former promise of publishing, as soon as our political affairs have assumed a still brighter aspect. [8]

Finally, in *The Psalm-Singer's Amusement* (1781), a more candid and desperate tone appears:

> This work is a part of the Book of Anthems, which I have so *LONG* promised, my Reasons for not publishing the whole in one Volumn [*sic*] must be obvious to all who consider the present extravagant price of Copper-Plate and Paper;—the Copper in special is so scarce, that I don't think it possible, to procure enough to contain the Whole, at any Price; besides if I was able to publish the Whole, but few would become Purchasers, and I believe, that the most will be of my Opinion, when I inform them, the book could not be afforded for less than *TEN DOLLARS.* However, I hope that notwithstanding the present Difficulties, I shall shortly be able to publish the Remainder at a much lower Price. [9]

Nothing more is heard of the original plan. "The Remainder" of those promised are undoubtedly part or all of the seventeen anthems included in Billings' last collection, *The Continental Harmony,* published in 1794.

Because of Billings' difficulties in issuing a unified collection, it is impossible to assign dates of composition to most of the anthems. No doubt some of those included in later books were finished before 1770. If that is so, they certainly underwent rather extensive revision before they finally appeared, for there is a great difference in musical style between the five works in *The New-England Psalm-Singer* (1770) and those of the "middle period" contained in *The Singing Master's Assistant* (1778), *The Psalm-Singer's Amusement* (1781), and *The Suffolk Harmony* (1786). A further, less

---

7. Billings, *New-England Psalm-Singer,* p. [2].
8. Billings, *Singing Master's Assistant,* p. [3].
9. Billings, *Psalm-Singer's Amusement,* p. 2.

obvious, development occurred during the eight years before the publication of *The Continental Harmony* in 1794.

An anthem representing each of these stages of musical evolution is included in the Musical Supplement: "As the hart panteth" (1770), "I love the Lord" (1778), and "I will love Thee, O Lord" (1794).

The growth of Billings' musicianship is traced in detail in the following survey of his style, a style founded upon the meager resources for self-instruction available to him, such as the Tufts and Walter books (see p. 14) and Tans'ur's *American Harmony* (see p. 41). The pervading influence of the latter collection, as erroneous and inadequate as it was, is clearly traceable in the theoretical introductions to Billings' own publications.

The typical anthem of the middle and late periods is a multisectional work lasting approximately five minutes. (Some are as short as two minutes; a few as long as ten or twelve.) The earlier works are more diffuse, more repetitious, and involve more passages in slower tempos, so that they are generally longer, requiring about eight or nine minutes of performance time.

All derive their structural basis from the text, with sectional divisions determined by successive sentences or verses. In the early works there is no clear musical demarcation of the different sections, and they might well be considered through-composed except for the numerous repetitions; but beginning in 1778 and continuing throughout Billings' creative life there is a continually increasing emphasis upon sectional contrast by means of musical devices such as changing meter, tempo, texture, or, occasionally, tonal center. Especially in the later works there is more evidence of a growing conception of musical form in the abstract sense of the term—recurrence of melodic motives throughout the piece or refrain-like repetition not suggested by the text in its original form.

The texts are derived from a variety of sources. The majority are selections from the Psalms in the King James Version, although an occasional turn of phrase reveals that the staunchly Congregational composer knew and preferred the Anglican Prayer Book version in some cases. Other Scriptural passages are used, as well as the Sternhold and Hopkins or Watts metrical Psalms, but most distinctive are the original passages—sometimes prose, sometimes verse—often containing direct references to contemporary life or events. The most notorious of this sort of thing is Billings' paraphrase of Psalm 137 beginning with "By the rivers of Watertown we sat down and wept when we remembered thee, O Boston." In a few cases the text is a potpourri derived admittedly "from sundry Scriptures and elsewhere" and intermingling passages from various books of the Bible, verses from hymns or metrical psalmody, and original material.

Even when ostensibly adhering to a single Psalm or Canticle, Billings follows the example set by Tans'ur and takes much the same sort of license in adding, omitting, substituting, or rearranging words and phrases. The text is generally set in a straightforward, syllabic style in which the normal qualitative and quantitative accent of the English words is preserved. There are frequent neumatic groupings of two, three, or four notes on one syllable, of course, and short melismas on some particularly poignant word are occasionally encountered. But, surprisingly, such florid passages are usually confined to choral sections, and the effect is minimized by words sounding simultaneously in another voice part. Nowhere does one find the very figurate solo melodies typical of the English composers.

All of Billings' anthems require a four-part mixed chorus. In only two of the forty-seven are there wordless passages marked "symphony." One of these is "O Thou to whom all creatures bow" in *The Continental Harmony,* where two short, two-part instrumental passages occur, one modulating from C major to F major, the other modulating back to C major at the end of the middle section. In *The Singing Master's Assistant,* published sixteen years previously, a "symphony" had been defined as "an air, which is played, or *sang without words* [italics mine] before the song begins, and sometimes such airs are in the middle of a piece and at the end."

The other anthem that calls for a "symphony" is the independent publication, "God is the King," called simply *Peace: An Anthem* on the title page. The only clue to the date of composition is the owner's inscription, "Ladd's [or Tadd's]. Newport. August 1783," on the front of the only surviving copy of the work, in the Brown University Library, Providence, Rhode Island. Judging from its length (above twelve minutes) and the extraordinary instrumental resources called for, it was probably intended for some special occasion. The title and a section of the text beginning "Rejoice, ye Americans, in the Lord" suggest some celebration or commemoration relating to the newly won independence of the former Colonies. That Billings was conscious of the unusual nature of the medium is evident from a footnote printed on the first page of the music wherein he felt obligated to explain that "Symphony is sounds without words intended for instruments."

In neither of the two pieces is there any really idiomatic instrumental writing.[10] Except for some impossibly high notes in the instrumental inter-

10. There is a closer relationship between the two pieces than the fact that both have instrumental parts. Measures 304–29 of "God is the king" are the same as the final twenty-five measures of the other anthem, with only minor harmonic differences.

ludes of "God is the king," the parts might well have been "sang without words." In the same piece the only function of the instruments (after a relatively long introduction) is to provide a very short interlude at the end of each section, usually a repetition of the last few measures of the vocal part just ended. It is assumed that the voice parts were doubled by the instruments; there is no independent accompaniment.

In almost all the anthems there are short passages for each of the parts alone, but there is evidence that Billings did not intend them for solo voices as did the English composers. In one of his instructional introductions, he warns the singers that "Much Caution should be used in singing a Solo, in my Opinion Two or Three at most are enough to sing it well, it should be sung as Soft as an Eccho. . . ." [11] The solo lines are even less figurate than some of the choral sections; there are none of the extended vehicles for florid vocal display sometimes encountered in the English product.

The growth of Billings' command of musical materials is most obvious in his handling of meter, rhythm, and harmony. Only one of the forty-seven anthems maintains a single time signature and tempo throughout the piece. In all the rest there are numerous changes of meter and tempo, ranging from one change to as many as twenty-one in "Was not the day dark and gloomy." As they do in the English works, the various time signatures indicate tempo as well as meter. In the early works Billings preferred the slower "moods of time," but beginning about 1780 there is a predominance of the faster movement ($\downarrow$ = M.M. 120) so closely identified with Billings and his disciples by the reformers of the last decade of the eighteenth century. The conventional Italian tempo designations (e.g., "Adagio," "Vivace,") are common in the early works but appear less frequently in each successive publication until they appear as an exception rather than the rule in *The Continental Harmony*.

The metric changes may occur at any time, and sometimes do occur with a frequency suggestive of the twentieth century. In "I heard a great voice" (1778), for example, measures 20–27 are marked successively $\frac{3}{2}$ $\frac{3}{2}$ $\frac{3}{2}$ $\frac{3}{2}$. In the later works, however, there is a tendency, not always followed, to confine metric changes to sectional divisions.

The reason for the many metric changes, particularly in the earlier works, seems to have been partly the composer's desire to imitate natural speech rhythms as closely as possible. Billings' concept of the pre-eminence of text over music is revealed in an exhortation to the singers in the introduction to *The Singing Master's Assistant* where he cautions that "Musical pronouncers must never sacrifice the sense, for the sake of softening the sound; but where the sense and the sound run counter to each other, the sound must give way." [12] Yet the probable real reason, Billings' failure to understand the basic principles of metric organization, often defeated his purpose.

The undeniable metric awkwardness of the early period results from the presence of textual accents, rhythmic patterns, and harmonic rhythms that contradict rather than ratify the written meter. A passage from "The Lord is King," with the actual meter indicated above the staff, illustrates these difficulties (Fig. 25).

A vast change and improvement is apparent in the anthems of *The Singing Master's Assistant*. Although some vestiges of the former difficul-

from: Billings, New England Psalm Singer, 1770, p. 29.

Fig. 25. Billings, "The Lord is King," mm. 105–11

ties remain, such as the awkward harmonic rhythm in measures 44–45 of "I love the Lord" (see Musical Supplement), the metric organization is much simpler, and there is the necessary co-ordination of textual, musical, and harmonic rhythms within the context of the chosen meter. By the 1780's there is often such complete correspondence of the various factors that "tyranny of the bar line" is the result.

There is little that is distinctive about Billings' rhythmic resources. With note values ranging from whole notes to sixteenth-notes, most patterns are comprised of half-, quarter-, or eighth-notes in simple relationships of adjacent values (i.e., a quarter-note will be followed by a half-note, an eighth-note, or another quarter-note). Dotted rhythms are used freely, however, and sometimes dominate the musical effects of a given passage.

Most of the rhythmic patterns are dictated, or at least suggested, by the

12. Billings, *Singing Master's Assistant*, p. 14.

text, but within sections a pattern may be reiterated for musical reasons until it achieves a measure of prominence. The only noteworthy deviations from this simple standard are the occasional triplet, "Scotch snap," and syncopated patterns. (See "I love the Lord," Musical Supplement.)

Billings' handling of harmonic materials reveals, even more clearly than the growing facility in metric organization, his development as a composer between 1770 and 1794. The harmonic idiom remains basically triadic throughout his creative period; the incidence of chords of the seventh (usually about 6 per cent of the total number of sonorities) does not increase, as one would expect, in the later works. But greater sonority and flexibility is attained by a gradual decrease in the number of incomplete triads (open fifths) and an increase in the proportion of inversions. The relative incidence of open fifths remains at approximately the same level during the early and middle periods (about 13 per cent), but in the later works the average occurrence is reduced to about 8 or 9 per cent of the chords sounded. In one case, "O God, Thou hast been displeased" (1794), there are only three open sonorities in the one hundred and fifty measures of music.

Only about 15 per cent of the triads in the early works are not in root position. The percentage of inversions (mostly first inversions) steadily increases to approximately 20 per cent in the middle period and about 25 per cent in the later works. The lowest percentage of inversions encountered was 12 per cent in the first setting of "Blessed is he that considereth the poor," and the highest was 33 per cent in "I will love Thee" (see Musical Supplement).

Unjustified dissonances—those which cannot be explained in terms of conventional non-harmonic tones—while never very numerous, appear with decreasing frequency in the successive publications. They are so rare in the anthems of 1794, in fact, that one is inclined to suspect printer's errors in those cases where they do occur.

The nature of the chord progressions is another telling index to Billings' musical evolution. The many modal and awkward progressions of the early period (e.g., root relationships of the interval of a second downward, such as V-IV, IV-III, III-II) are gradually replaced by the more conventional relationships of a third, fourth, or fifth up or down. Even in the later works, however, enough of the archaic progressions and a notably high proportion of secondary triads remain to furnish an interestingly anomalous flavor to the harmonic vocabulary.

Several harmonic progressions occur with sufficient regularity to warrant identification as Billings mannerisms. The cadential formula, II_6-IV^7-V-I, a cliché of the period, was a particular favorite (see Musical Supplement, "I love the Lord," mm. 62–63). More distinctive of Billings are the patterns identified by J. Murray Barbour, in an unpublished essay, as the "Greensleeves" progression and the "Summer Canon" progression (Fig. 26).

Two rather striking harmonic devices, more conspicuous by virtue of their rarity, are the ending of a minor section on a major triad (*Tierce de Picardie*) and an extended phrase without harmonic or melodic movement which produces a psalmodic, chantlike effect. Neither of these devices occurs in any other eighteenth-century work, English or American, published in the Colonies; they were either original with Billings or imitations of some unknown models.

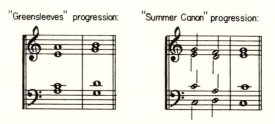

FIG. 26. "Greensleeves" and "Summer Canon" progressions

The whole harmonic vocabulary is patently diatonic. In the early works there is no chromatic alteration except an occasional raised seventh scale step in the minor mode, but secondary dominants (limited to V of V, V of VI or, rarely, V of III) and a very infrequent alteration involving a raised fourth scale step appear in the middle and late periods. Billings' inept handling of this "new" effect is amusing at first when he introduces a V of V, for, example, and resolves it not to the dominant but to the tonic. In the late works the treatment is more orthodox.

Billings' cadential structure is an enigma. Usually a few cadential formulas are adopted by the composers of an era and become conventionalized if not tacitly inviolable. But Billings vacillates freely between various forms of the authentic cadence: most commonly V-I° or V-I; less frequently V°-I, V°-I°, V_7-I or $V_7°$-I. A single anthem may include several different types, although there is generally a preponderance of one progression in a given work. The expected evolution from formulas involving incomplete triads in the early pieces to complete authentic cadences in the later ones does not occur. The two most common types are found equally throughout the works.

Harmonic rhythm, which produced some of the metric difficulties described above, is generally fast; a contrast of pace is sometimes achieved by slowing the frequency of harmonic change, and occasionally the special effect of static harmony is introduced. Chord spacing may be either wide or close, depending upon the tessitura of the tenor part.

One tonal center is usually maintained throughout an anthem. C major and G major are the preferred keys, but a good many of the pieces are in a minor mode. Fluctuation between the major (or "sharp key") and minor ("flat key") forms of the same tonal center are common, as are transitory excursions to the relative major or minor key. The minor keys, particularly in the early works, have a strong modal flavor as a result of many V and VII chords without the raised seventh scale step.

In only two of the forty-seven works is a real modulation effected. In "O Thou to whom all creatures bow" two sections in F major are separated by a middle part in C major. The other instance, "O God, Thou hast been displeased" (1794), seems to have been Billings' grand experiment in tonal manipulation. Beginning in G minor, the tonal center veers through B-flat major, C major, C minor, E-flat major, C minor, C major, C minor, E-flat major, C minor, E-flat major, F major, F minor, and C major before being reined in F major!

The prevailing texture in all Billings' anthems is a four-part, homophonic "familiar style" with the melody assigned to the tenor part. Sometimes there is a reduction to only two or three parts, and the monophonic solos furnish further variety. Another genre of homophony, to be distinguished from the note-against-note, chordal type, is the melody-with-accompaniment style illustrated in the closing "Hallelujah" section of "As the hart panteth" (see Musical Supplement); it is achieved by opposing one moving part to obviously subordinate material in the accompanying voices.

One other exception to the four-part standard must be noted because of its frequent appearance. Even in the earliest works, *divisi* parts are encountered in the treble, counter, and bass lines. They are never in the tenor part. Billings explains them in the introduction to *The Singing Master's Assistant:* "When you meet with two or three Notes standing one over the other, they are called Choosing Notes, and signify that you may sing which you please, or all if your part has performers enough, and remember that they add not to the time; but to the Variety." [13] The increased sonority is always brief, often limited to one or two chords, but Billings must be given credit for originality because the device is rarely found in the models known to have been available to him.

Within this primarily homophonic context, almost every anthem has some

13. Billings, *Singing Master's Assistant,* p. [16].

polyphonic aspect, usually one or two sections of "fuguing" music inserted as textural variety. This polyphony may be any of three basic types found in the English and American anthems of the period: imitative, non-imitative, or textual.

from: Billings, New England Psalm Singer, 1770, p. 83.

FIG. 27. Billings, "Hear my prayer," mm. 58–63

All degrees of strictness and freedom are represented in the imitative sections. Some have fugue-like real and tonal answers at the fifth and octave as in the passage from "Hear my prayer" in Figure 27. In others there is a

from: Billings, Singing Master's Assistant, 1778, p. 74.

FIG. 28. Billings, "I am the Rose of Sharon," mm. 32–35

mere suggestion of imitation which is discarded almost immediately (see Fig. 28).

Regarding the emphasis to be given to successive entries in either imitative or non-imitative polyphony, Billings warns singers that "in performing Pieces where your part is sometimes silent; after you have beat your empty

Bars, you must fall in with *spirit;* because that gives the Audience to understand another part is added which perhaps they would not be so sensible of, if you struck in soft." [14]

More frequent than the orthodox points of imitation are passages wherein the different parts maintain independent melodic and rhythmic interest but make no attempt at imitation. An example of this type, with the further distinction of being in "duet style," is the closing "Hallelujah" section of "I will Love Thee" (see Musical Supplement). This type was also "fuguing music" to Billings; as he explained in the list of definitions in *The Singing Master's Assistant:*

> FUGE, or Fuging—Notes flying after each other, altho' not always the same sound. N.B. Music is said to be Fuging, when on part comes in after another; its beauties cannot be numbered, it is sufficient to say, that it is universally pleasing.
>
> IMITATION—Is when one part imitates, or mimicks another. N.B. This is frequently done in Fuging pieces. [15]

The unique overlapping of the solo parts in the first section of "As the hart panteth" (Musical Supplement, mm. 10–15, 18) is an unorthodox practice, even for Billings. It would be interesting to know if he considered the device "fuguing" in 1770.

The third type, textual polyphony, is actually a pseudo-polyphony in that there is little or no rhythmic and melodic independence. The same practice has been noted previously in the anthems of Knapp (see p. 60). Only the simultaneous sounding of different portions of the text by the different voices conveys the impression of the predominance of horizontal over vertical conception. The example from "My friends, I am going" (Fig. 29) illustrates an obvious form of textual polyphony as well as a string of first inversions reminiscent of fauxbourdon—and of William Selby (see p. 87). When, as often happens, there is a bit more independence among the parts, the distinction between this and the second (non-imitative) type of polyphony becomes a matter of the degree of independence. All three types share certain characteristics: they function as a means of textural variety, they are relatively brief, and they soon dissolve into the more common chordal idiom.

If one expects a gradual evolution between 1770 and 1794 from rudimentary melodic independence to the more demanding strict imitation, one is again disappointed. There is no discernible pattern in the development of

14. *Ibid.*, p. [13].
15. *Ibid.*, p. [25].

Billings' contrapuntal technique. In the early works are found points of imitation neither more nor less skillfully contrived than those of the 1790's. This circumstance may be a result of the belated publication of anthems implied by the announcements quoted above (p. 106). One less significant aspect of texture should be noted. Occasional responsorial or antiphonal exchanges sometimes occur, but they are in the nature of special effects rather than common practices.

Of all the musical elements, Billings' melodic style is the most elusive of definition. Most of the melodies are simple, straightforward, lyric tunes conceived as expressive vehicles for the words at hand; and most are very

from: Billings, Continental Harmony, 1790, p. 166.

Fig. 29. Billings, "My friends, I am going," mm. 43–45

effective in fulfilling that criterion. There are occasional passages with a strong flavor of intrinsic "tunefulness"—in the folksong sense—such as the tenor part in measures 90–106 of "As the hart panteth" (see Musical Supplement), but irregularity of phrase length usually minimizes this factor.

Billings' years as a singing teacher are reflected in his consideration of the range limitations of the various parts. Trebles are usually confined to the octave from g' to g''; counters to a seventh, from c' to b''. Tenors, as the melodic part, normally range from f in the bass clef up to g' or a''—a ninth or a tenth. The bass part is the most demanding, averaging about a twelfth down from middle c'. The range limits of the bass part are somewhat hard to define because of Billings' practice, again considerate, of writing many notes in octaves so that each singer could choose his comfortable tessitura. Considering these octave "choosing notes," the bass parts cover a phenomenal range from low C to d' above middle c'. Billings' own ideal disposition of voices on the parts was, fortunately for us, recorded in the introduction to *The Singing Master's Assistant*:

If a man sings a tenor with a masculine and a woman with a feminine voice, the tenor is as full as two parts and a tune so sung (although it has but four parts) is in effect the same as six. Such a conjunction of masculine and feminine voices is beyond expression sweet and ravishing. . . . we ought to take grateful notice, that the Author of Harmony has so curiously constructed our Organs, that there are about three or four deep voices suitable for the Bass to one for the upper parts, which is about the proportion required in the laws of Harmony. . . .[16]

The length of the melodic lines varies according to the nature of the text and, consequently, the tempo. They are sometimes impossibly long, as in the phrase from "The Lord descended" quoted in Figure 30, and

from: Billings, New England Psalm Singer, 1770, p.52.

Fig. 30. Billings, "The Lord descended," mm. 34–44 (tenor part)

sometimes motival, short-breathed phrases such as those found in measures 116–34 of "I will love Thee, O Lord" (see Musical Supplement), but most are neither distinctively long nor short.

Melodic progression is basically stepwise (except for the bass part in its harmonic function), but there is a notable frequency of harmonic motivation in outlining triads (e.g., the opening measures of "I will love Thee"). Sequential organization appears in works of all periods (see Fig. 30).

Except for one trill on the penultimate note of "Blessed is he that considereth the poor" (1770), written melodic ornamentation is confined to a little figuration in melismatic passages. The figure in measures 32–33 of "I will love Thee" illustrates a typical usage and, at the same time, another direct derivation from Tans'ur (see p. 56).

In addition to the relatively small amount of written ornamentation, there seems to have been a considerable improvised melodic decoration in the tradition of Renaissance "diminution." In the instructional introductions to the first two collections Billings refers to the "Grace of Transition" which "if rightly performed, is one of the greatest Ornaments to Music that can be used; and in my Opinion, the turning of thirds up and down, is one of the

16. *Ibid.*, pp. 14–15.

nicest Points, and if well done, beautifies the music exceedingly, whether Vocal or Instrumental." [17] Although the verbal description is ambiguous, the illustrative examples in *The Singing Master's Assistant* reveal the nature of the practice (Fig. 31).

Grace of Transition

from: Billings, <u>Singing Master's Assistant</u>, 1778, p. 103.

FIG. 31. "Grace of Transition"

In another passage in the same book, Billings describes a less gratifying performance practice:

> N.B. Many ignorant Singers take great licence from these Trills, and without confining themselves to any rule, they shake all notes promiscuously, and they are apt to tear a note in pieces, which should be struck fair and plump, as any other. Let such persons be informed that . . . they must not shake any note but what is marked with a Trill, and that according to the rule.[18]

The "rule" is then illustrated for the guidance of the transgressors (Fig. 32).

from: Billings, <u>Singing Master's Assistant</u>, 1778, p. (7).

FIG. 32. A single trill and a double trill

Billings exhibits little conception of the coloristic possibilities of the mixed chorus, but, in doing so, he was simply mirroring the aesthetic of an age that emphasized line over color values in graphic arts as well as music. Rather than coloristic effects, numerous and frequent changes of texture served to inject a vital variety into the sound mass.

In the same way, little exploitation is made of dynamic contrast. Surprisingly, dynamic markings such as "forte," "fortissimo," and "piano" are

17. Billings, *New-England Psalm-Singer*, p. [16].
18. Billings, *Singing Master's Assistant*, p. [7].

much more frequently encountered in the early period than in the middle or later works. In a great majority of the seventeen anthems in *The Continental Harmony* there is no dynamic indication of any kind. The same is true of such expressive suggestions as "Vigoroso," "Lamentatone," "Divoto," "Grave," "Affetuoso," and "Languissiant." It seems strange that Billings should have grown less concerned with musical expressiveness as his technique developed.

"Madrigalisms" play an effective, but not primary, role among Billings' musical effects; the descriptive devices in "I will love Thee" are typical: the figuration on the word "shake" in measures 32–33, the descending melodic line on "and come down" in measures 47–48, and the wonderfully thunderous "thunder" in measure 92.

It becomes apparent, after thoughtful analysis of the music, that such arbitrary pronouncements as that Billings' music "has, of course, only historical interest" or is "musically worthless" are not only superficial but completely unjust and erroneous. The impression of Billings as an eccentric musical oaf is too widely circulated by those who know only the early works, those who magnify the admitted faults, or those who really do not know the music at all. Many anthems of Billings' middle and later periods have the charm of enthusiasm and originality, but, more important, they are intrinsically attractive as music and compare very favorably with reputable English products of the same period.

Thirteen years elapsed after Billings' *New-England Psalm-Singer* before an anthem by a second New England composer appeared in print. In 1783 an "Anthem from Sundry Parts of Revelations by Benham" was published in Oliver Brownson's *Select Harmony*. Before the end of that decade Billings and Benham were joined by five more native composers: in chronological order of first publication, Jacob French, Abraham Wood, Daniel Read, Carpenter, and Frost.

ASAHEL BENHAM

Asahel Benham, born in New Hartford, Connecticut, in 1757, traveled around New England and the Middle Atlantic States as a teacher of singing schools, where his success seems to have stemmed more from his impressive appearance and personal integrity than from his musical qualifications. Benham compiled two collections of church music, *The Federal Harmony* (six editions between 1790 and 1796) and *The Social Harmony* (1798). Both were issued in Connecticut, the former in New Haven and Middletown. The Preface to the latter collection was dated at Wallingford,

September 6, 1798; so it may be that the composer settled there late in life. He died in 1805.

Benham's anthem, "Holy, Holy, Holy, Lord God Almighty," which appeared in the two editions (1783 and 1791) of the Brownson collection, is the only one known to have been composed by him. It was also included in the 1790 and 1792 editions of the anonymous *Federal Harmony*, but did not appear in either of Benham's own publications. Only two anthems, one by Justin Morgan and one by Jacob French, were included in the various editions of Benham's *Federal Harmony*. The one selection bearing that designation in *The Social Harmony* is an anonymous "Hiram Anthem: Psalm 133," which is simply a psalm tune. The editors and compilers of tune collections were usually careful in their application of the term "anthem"; the reason for its use in Benham's collection is not apparent.

Stylistically, "Holy, Holy, Holy, Lord God Almighty" adheres closely to Billings' early works. There is the same difficulty in reconciling textual, harmonic, and musical rhythms with the chosen meter, and the same primitive harmonic vocabulary. In fact, there is an even larger proportion of open fifths (about 20 per cent) than Billings employed. To Benham's credit are the less diffuse form—it is about four minutes long with sectional divisions clearly demarcated—and a more skillful handling of contrapuntal texture in the few instances where it is introduced. In measures 82–88, for

from: Brownson, Select Harmony, 1783, pp. 67-8.

Fig. 33. Benham, "Holy, Holy, Holy," mm. 82–88.

example, two canons are carried on simultaneously—one between bass and counter, and one between treble and tenor (Fig. 33). These creditable factors hardly compensate for the harmonic and metric deficiencies, however. The work is of little significance in the development of the anthem in New England and is of small value in terms of modern performance.

JACOB FRENCH

In the same Brownson collection that contained Benham's anthem, a third New England composer was introduced for the first time—Jacob French. The only documented facts relating to French's life are those found in the records of the town of Stoughton, Massachusetts, where he was born on July 15, 1754, the second child of Jacob and Miriam Downs French.[19] He may have lived there at least until 1779 when he married Miss Esther Neale of that town on May 26, although he probably would be listed among the students in Billings' singing school in 1774 had he been in Stoughton at the time. Any knowledge of his whereabouts and activities after his marriage must be derived from his three published collections of church music: *The New American Melody* (1789) which gives his home as Medway, Massachusetts; *The Psalmodist's Companion*, published by Isaiah Thomas in Worcester in 1793; and *The Harmony of Harmony*, issued in Northampton, Massachusetts, in 1802. A helpful clue appeared in the "Advertisement" of the second of the three books, where French refers to himself as "having been many years a teacher of Music."

The list of anthems and publications in Table 6 shows that only one ("My friends, I am going") of French's nine anthems attained any measure of popularity. It is a peculiar reflection upon the taste of the locale and era that this anthem, the first by the composer, should have been singled out for approval by the singers. Of the nine, it is the shortest, the simplest, and the most elementary in its harmonic, tonal, and textural schemes. There are many more open fifths and more archaic harmonic progressions than in the others, and the non-imitative polyphony of the opening sections is obviously the work of a beginner. The picturesque, if somewhat lugubrious, text may account for its appeal.

More properly representative of French's style is "O sing unto the Lord" (see Musical Supplement). This anthem, published in 1789, shows a remarkable similarity in style to that of Billings during the 1790's. It is obvious that French matured as a musician much more rapidly than did his

19. Metcalf, *op. cit.*, pp. 88–89.

better-known colleague. In fact, some details of his style (for example, the rudimentary attempts at harmonic and melodic chromaticism in measures 26–28 and 45–47 of "O sing unto the Lord") surpass anything that Billings ever attempted. The VII chord with a raised fifth in measure 46 is an instance of French's favorite device of chromatic alteration.

TABLE 6

PUBLICATION IN NEW ENGLAND OF ANTHEMS BY JACOB FRENCH

Descend from heav'n, celestial dove (12) *
Hear, O heav'ns, and give ear, O earth (12)
I beheld and lo (3)
Lift up your heads (12)
My friends, I am going (1–2, 4, 5–9, 10, 11–13)
Now after these things (4)
O sing unto the Lord (4, 14)
Righteous art Thou, O Lord (4)
The Song of Songs is Solomon's (10) †
Why dost thou sit solitary (4)

Date	Publication	Number of Anthems
1. 1783	Brownson, *Select Harmony*, 1st ed.	1
2. 1791	The same, 2d ed.	1
3. 1786	*Worcester Collection*	1
4. 1789	French, *New American Melody*	5
5. 1792	Benham, *Federal Harmony*, 2d ed.	1
6. 1793	The same, 3d ed.	1
7. 1794	The same, 4th ed.	1
8. 1795	The same, 5th ed.	1
9. 1796	The same, 6th ed.	1
10. 1793	French, *Psalmodist's Companion*	2
11. 1796	*Village Harmony*, 2d ed.	1
12. 1797	The same, 3d ed.	1
13. 1798	The same, 4th ed.	1
14. 1802	French, *Harmony of Harmony*	4

* See note to Table 1 for explanation of numbers in parentheses.

† "The Song of Songs is Solomon's" appears only in *The Psalmodist's Companion*, where no composers are named. Another anthem in the same collection is identified as French's when it is included in a later collection. For that reason, and on the basis of stylistic similarity, "The Song of Songs is Solomon's" is herein ascribed to French.

Although "O sing unto the Lord" contains more features of French's style than any other one of his anthems, there are a few atypical aspects which should be pointed out. First, there are no solo parts present; French usually includes short solo passages for bass, tenor, or treble. Second, there are no feminine endings or ties across the bar line which sometimes produce a sense of metric irregularity or unbalance. Third, there is no melodic ornamentation in the form of melismatic figuration. Fourth, the 9/4 metric signature of the last three measures is unique; it was not used in any other anthem published in New England during the eighteenth century. All other characteristics—the tonal fluctuation between major and minor on the same key note, the high incidence of seventh chords and inversions, the antiphonal effects in duet style, the non-imitative polyphonic insertions, and the primary concern with a straightforward, effective setting of the Psalm text—are characteristic of French. Most of the anthems are attractive and would be useful additions to the repertory of a modern choral group.

ABRAHAM WOOD

In 1784, a year following the first publications of Benham and French, Abraham Wood issued an independent publication, *A Hymn on Peace.* [20] Wood was a lifelong resident of Northboro, Massachusetts, and "one of its prominent citizens and officials." [21] Born on July 30, 1752, he became a fuller, or dresser of cloth, by trade and died of apoplexy in Northboro on August 6, 1804. He served as clerk and drummer in the militia company of which his brother was captain during the Revolution, and he was himself captain of a reserve company for many years after the war. Different from most of the other American anthem composers, he seems not to have been a teacher of singing schools. His recorded musical activity, aside from composition and publication of church music, was limited to singing in the choir of his church in Northboro. Other publications besides the anthem mentioned above were *Divine Songs*, a collection of hymn tunes issued in 1789, *The Columbian Harmony* (1793, in collaboration with Joseph Stone) and *A Funeral Elegy on the Death of . . . George Washington* (1800).

Although very prolific as a composer of psalm and hymn tunes, Wood produced only two anthems. An independent publication of an anthem—not a part of a collection—was unusual in New England during the period under consideration, and so it would be rewarding to know the circumstances that brought about Wood's issuing the *Hymn on Peace* ("Behold array'd in

20. On the title page it is identified as *A Hymn on Peace*, but newspaper advertisements called it *An Anthem on Peace*.

21. Metcalf, *op. cit.*, p. 84.

light"), his first known publication of any kind. The second of his two anthems, "Where shall we go to seek and find," appeared only in *The Columbian Harmony.*

The surprising feature of the two works is that the one published in 1793 is notably less musically "correct" than the one published nine years earlier. It is possible, of course, that the later piece was written before "Behold array'd in light," but if that were so, one would expect some revision and correction before publication.

The inferiority of "Where shall we go to seek and find" is apparent in the conflict between the meter and the textual and harmonic rhythms, in several unjustified harmonic dissonances, and in the rudimentary character of the one short (four measures) polyphonic insertion. All these deficiencies are remedied in "Behold array'd in light," where the total effect compares favorably with Billings' later style. There is nothing really distinctive about either work except, possibly, the several trills, the low C for basses, and the plagal final cadence in "Where shall we go." Both are settings of metrical verse; the first is a hymn and the second a version of Psalm 132.

DANIEL READ

Daniel Read was the most active composer and promoter of church music in Connecticut during the eighteenth century. Born in Rehoboth, Massachusetts, on November 16, 1757, he settled in New Haven in 1799 as a partner of engraver Amos Doolittle in the business of book publishing and selling.[22] Although the partnership did not last long—Read became proprietor of a general merchandise store—he continued compiling and publishing collections of music as an avocation until his death in New Haven in 1836.

According to popular tradition, Read began composing tunes when only seventeen years of age (1774), but his first publication was *The American Singing Book* in 1785 (six editions before 1796). This was followed by *An Introduction to Psalmody* (1790); *The Columbian Harmonist, No. I* (1793); *The Columbian Harmonist, No. II* (1794); *The Columbian Harmonist, No. III* (1795; the three were combined and issued as a unified

---

22. Metcalf, *op. cit.*, pp. 94–99. A little-known, but extremely valuable, additional source of information are two of Read's notebooks which contain the first drafts of all letters written by Read during the periods 1793–1807 and 1829–32. Now in the New Haven Colony Historical Society, they are described by Irving Lowens in "Daniel Read's World: The Letters of an Early American Composer," *Notes of the Music Library Association,* ser. 2, IX (March, 1952), 233–48.

collection at the same time); and *The New Haven Collection of Sacred Music* (1817). His last collection, completed in 1832 and presented to the American Home Missionary Society with the request that funds derived from its sale be applied to the work of the society, was never published. Containing over four hundred tunes, the manuscript is now in the library of the New Haven Colony Historical Society.

As an anthem composer, Read belongs wholly to the eighteenth century, although he continued writing hymn tunes during the nineteenth. His six known anthems were published in the collections named above: "Down steers the bass" and "O praise the Lord, O my soul" in *The American Singing Book* (1785); "Hear our prayer, O Lord," "I know that my Redeemer lives," "It is better to go to the house of mourning," and "O be joyful in the Lord" in *The Columbian Harmonist, No. III* (1795). To this list should be added Read's version of the recitative, "There were shepherds abiding in the fields," combined with Handel's "Glory to God" in the latter collection (see pp. 92–93). Counting all editions of the former collection (there were other editions of the latter in the nineteenth century), there were seventeen instances of publication of an anthem by Read.

The most distinctive feature of the musical style of Read's anthems is its inconsistency. Although the pieces are generally rather short, they range in style from the simple, hymnlike "It is better to go to the house of mourning" to the very progressive and colorful "O be joyful in the Lord," from a rather "home-made" harmonic scheme in the former to a completely conventional idiom in the latter. Since no one of the works can serve as a composite picture of his style, "O be joyful in the Lord," his best work, represents Read in the Musical Supplement.

Several features of the work are noteworthy: the first, of course, is the optional instrumental accompaniment to the counter (alto) solo beginning at measure 63. Not only is the combination very rare, but it is also one of the few bits of concrete evidence that instruments were used. Even without the instruments, the length alone of the solo is unusual in an American work. And the effective "sigh" suspensions (e.g., m. 61) suggest that the composer was familiar with European music of the same period. The prominence given polyphonic texture in the opening and closing sections is also unique among Read's works, and not common among any of his contemporaries. The canonic imitation between the treble and tenor in measures 95–114, combined with a free part for the counter, is evidence of some skill in contrapuntal writing, even though Read failed to produce an orthodox point of imitation in any of his music.

Two other striking features are the concern for choral color manifest in the unison passage in measures 41–43, and the final plagal cadence—one of the three deviations from the basic authentic cadence in the whole American anthem repertory of the eighteenth century.

Finally, as identification of Read's model in choral writing, the Adagio section (mm. 49 ff.) should be compared with the passage beginning with "The kingdom of this world" in the "Hallelujah Chorus" from the *Messiah*. It is not surprising that the composer named one of his sons George Frederick Handel Read.

Nothing—not even their first names—is known about the other two composers whose works were included in publications of the 1780's. Each appears as the composer of one anthem, and is never heard of again. In the first (1786) and third (1791) editions of *The Worcester Collection*, an "Anthem to Funeral Thought" is attributed to a composer identified only as "Frost," and a setting of "Sing, O daughter of Zion" by one "Carpenter" was included in Chauncey Langdon's *The Beauties of Psalmody* (1786), compiled for the use of the Musical Society of Yale College. Twenty years later, in 1805, Rufus Frost compiled and published a collection called *The Medford Harmony*, which contained one anthem by the compiler. There is a remote possibility that the Frost represented in *The Worcester Collection* is the same man, but the vast difference in style between the two works makes it very improbable. If the birth date of Rufus Frost were known, it would be possible to ascertain if he *could* have written the earlier work, but he, too, is known only through his publication.

The anonymity of both Frost and Carpenter is well deserved. Both works are short and simple, no more musically demanding than some of the hymn tunes in the same books. In fact, the Frost piece is a setting of four verses of one of Dr. Watts's hymns ("Hark! from the tombs a doleful sound"), but the designation "anthem" is justified because different music is provided for each verse. The harmonic vocabulary of both anthems is characterized by a high percentage of open fifths, a low incidence of seventh chords and inversions, and predominantly "ungrateful" chord progressions. The texture of both is a chordal "familiar style" with the exception of one non-imitative "fuguing" section in the Carpenter piece. The one notable feature of Frost's "Hark! from the tombs" is the unsuccessful, but interesting, attempt at chromaticism illustrated in measures 5–7 of Figure 34.

Thirteen more New Englanders joined the ranks of anthem composers during the last decade of the eighteenth century, adding about fifty more works to the fast-growing repertory of singing schools and choirs. The

from: Worcester Collection, 1786, p. 182.

FIG. 34. Frost, "Hark! from the tombs," mm. 1–8

contributions of each will be described in the following pages in chronological order of first publication.

JUSTIN MORGAN

In each of the six editions of Benham's *Federal Harmony* issued between 1790 and 1796, there appeared the one known anthem of Justin Morgan. Much more famous as the breeder of the original Morgan horse than as a composer, Morgan was born in West Springfield, Massachusetts, in 1747. Because of delicate health, he did not follow the farming tradition of his family but devoted his life to teaching singing schools, grammar schools, and—in a time when fine penmanship was a source of pride—writing schools. In Springfield, where he remained until moving to Randolph, Vermont, in 1788, he also ran a tavern and conducted a small-scale business in horse-breeding. In Randolph he was the town clerk in addition to the teaching activities, which he continued until his death on March 2, 1798.

His many "fuguing-tunes," his imaginative, if untutored, musicianship, his originality, and his attraction to texts of a somewhat vivid pictorial quality (e.g., ". . . while the living worm lies gnawing within them") are all strongly reminiscent of William Billings. Another similarity to his better-known contemporary is an implied patriotism in his disdain of Italian tempo and dynamics markings; he used only English indications such as "slow," "lively," "soft," and "very loud."

The most remarkable feature of "Hark, you mortals, hear the trumpet" is its tonal gravitation between two unrelated key centers in the following order: E minor, E-flat major, E minor, E-flat major, E minor, E-flat major. There is no pretense at modulation; one section simply ends in one key, and the next begins in the other key with the result that one of the parts may be called upon to accomplish the feat of finding, for example, a dominant B-natural after ending on a tonic E-flat.

Two coloristic devices, apparently original with Morgan, occur several times during the course of the anthem. One is a sudden change of tessitura for the sake of graphic expressiveness (see Fig. 35). The other is achieved by having one or two voices continue to sound after the others have dropped out of a four-part chord (mm. 55–56 in Fig. 35).

from: Benham, Federal Harmony, 1795, pp. 43–45.

Fig. 35. Morgan, "Hark, you mortals," mm. 13–17, 54–58

Unfortunately, these very attractive aspects of the piece are hobbled by a rude harmonic scheme (almost half the sonorities are open fifths), some contradiction between meter and harmonic rhythm, and the doggerel character of the text.

THOMAS LEE, JR.

About the same time that Morgan's anthem first appeared, another collection of psalm tunes, "principally the production of American Authors," was published (in Boston?) by Daniel Willard and Thomas Lee, Jr. Entitled *Sacred Harmony* (1790), the volume contained, in addition to the usual rudimentary instruction in musical fundamentals and sixty-one psalm tunes, two anthems: "Behold how good and how pleasant" and "Hark! Suddenly bursting o'er our heads." The composer of the former is identified as one of the publishers, Thomas Lee, Jr., and the latter appears to be anonymous. Nothing is known about Lee's life and activities.

Because of the great similarity in style of the two works—especially the peculiar and distinctive harmonic idiom—either both were written by Lee, or one served as the model for the other. Both the pieces are rather short, straightforward settings of Psalm texts for four-part mixed chorus, and both have the same tonal plan—beginning in A minor and modulating soon to C major. There are two polyphonic insertions in "Hark! Suddenly bursting o'er our heads" where the voices enter in succession, but both passages return to chordal treatment at the end of four measures.

The primitive harmonic idiom, with its many dissonances and awkward progressions, reveals that Lee had had little, if any, training and probably accounts for the fact that only one of the two works was published a second time. "Behold how good and how pleasant" appeared in Griswold and Skinner's *Connecticut Harmony*, which is assigned to 1796 by Evans and to *ca.* 1800 by Metcalf.

The versatile Mr. Lee is named as the engraver as well as the composer of "Behold how good and how pleasant" in *Sacred Harmony*. It is unfortunate, in the interests of the present study, that he should have been far more skillful in the former craft.

OLIVER HOLDEN

With the anthems of Oliver Holden a high point is reached in the eighteenth-century development of the form in New England. Holden was born in Shirley, Massachusetts, on September 18, 1765, and thus belongs to the second generation of American composers. He had only a few months of common school education in Groton, but a lively intellect and an adventurous spirit enabled him to qualify as the clerk for the construction company engaged to erect the first Boston-Charlestown bridge in 1785. Meanwhile, before he was twenty, he had been a cabinet-maker's apprentice in Grafton, a farmer in Groton and Pepperrell, a Revolutionary soldier (at sixteen), a sailor on a commercial frigate, and a teacher of singing schools—after only two months of formal instruction in the rudiments of music.

In Charlestown, where he remained until his death in 1844, he operated a real estate business, was a carpenter, ran a music store, founded and served as minister of the "Puritan Church," and was very active in civil affairs.[23] In his own words:

23. Metcalf, *op. cit.*, pp. 124–34.

From the age of twenty-one to seventy-seven I have been in public life—most of the time in business for the Town as Selectman, Assessor, Collector, Overseer of the Poor and many years Representative to the Legislature; and from five of our Governors I have had Commissions as Justice—the last of which I now hold unexpired, from my dear Friend, and at times, fellow-citizen Edward Everett.

And here ends the nauceous egotism.[24]

A very prolific composer and publisher of church music—for which he is still remembered because of the tune "Coronation," usually sung to the words "All hail the power of Jesus' name"—Holden issued seven collections,[25] and served as editor of an eighth during the decade between 1792 and 1803. In addition to those listed in Table 7, there were *The Massachusetts Compiler* (1795, in collaboration with Hans Gram and Samuel Holyoke) and *The Charlestown Collection of Sacred Songs*, published in 1803.

In addition to the twelve anthems listed in Table 7, Holden composed a good many occasional pieces which he designated as "ode," "dirge," "hymn," or "poem." These pieces are identical in musical style to the anthems but are not included in the present survey because of the secular nature of their texts.

As early as Holden's first publication in 1792, one can sense that he is not in complete sympathy with the vigorous, lively style of church music prevalent during the last thirty years of the eighteenth century. In the Preface to *The American Harmony* he advises the singers:

> With respect to the manner of performing the Music, the Author wishes that the time in general might be slow, and the strains soft. Doubtless singing Choirs, in general, are too inattentive to these important parts of Music. By hurrying a piece of Music, performers are more likely to sing harsh; in consequence of which, good pronunciation is lost.[26]

The Preface to *The Union Harmony*, published in the following year, is even more direct, although he recognizes the effectiveness of polyphony for certain purposes:

> Fuging music in general is badly calculated for divine worship; for it often happens that music of this description will not admit of a change of

24. Manuscript autobiographical letter from Oliver Holden to George Hood, [1842], now in the Music Department of the Boston Public Library.
25. *The Modern Collection,* an anonymous publication of 1800, is also usually attributed to Holden. The anthem content is practically identical with that of *The Union Harmony.*
26. Holden, *American Harmony*, p. [2].

words without injuring the subject. In such cases it would be better to reject the tune, than to obscure, or injure the words; but, when a tune is so contrived as to admit of changing the words with propriety, the parts falling in by turn serve to convey the meaning and impress the importance of the words more forcibly than otherwise they would, especially if the subject be praise.[27]

TABLE 7

PUBLICATION IN NEW ENGLAND OF ANTHEMS BY OLIVER HOLDEN

As the hart panteth (7) *
Great is the Lord (8)
Hear my cry, O God (2)
How amiable are Thy tabernacles (3)
I will praise Thee, O Lord (5)
Listen, O isles, unto me (7)
The Lord is good to all (1)
The Lord reigneth (1)
Man that is born of woman (3–4, 5–6)
O Thou that hearest prayer (1)
Sing, O ye heavens (1)
The sound of the harp ceaseth (9)

	Date	Publication	Number of Anthems
1.	1792	Holden, *American Harmony*	4
2.	1793	Holden, *Union Harmony*	1
3.	1796	The same, 2d ed.	2
4.	1801	The same, 3d ed.	1
5.	1797	Holden (ed.), *Worcester Collection*, 6th ed.	2
6.	1800	The same, 7th ed.	1
7.	[1800]	Holden, *Occasional Pieces*	2
8.	1800	Holden, *Plain Psalmody*	1
9.	[1800]	Holden, *Sacred Dirges*	1

* See note to Table 1 for explanation of numbers in parentheses.

Finally, in *Plain Psalmody* a reference in the "Advertisement" unequivocally establishes Holden in the vanguard of the reaction against the Billings school—of those who favored a quieter, more devotional type of church music. "In the general omission of fuges, the Author hopes to meet the approbation and concurrence of the lovers of real devotion."[28]

27. Holden, *Union Harmony*, pp. iii–iv.
28. Holden, *Plain Psalmody*, p. [2].

This restraint is evident not only in Holden's congregational tunes but in his anthems as well. "The Lord is good to all" (see Musical Supplement), has a metric signature of 2/4, the quickest "mood of common time," and a favorite of Billings', but there is a significant qualification in the indication "Moderato," which meant that "the strain should be performed at least one third slower." [29]

Most of Holden's musical characteristics are present in the anthem. The metric-rhythmic scheme is simple and free of the contradictions that troubled many of his contemporaries. The melodic line is a lyric, expressive vehicle for the text, yet not devoid of grateful effects such as the melismatic figuration in measures 39–40 and "sigh" suspensions (m. 30)—effects that are intrinsically musical as distinguished from those motivated by textual considerations. Although there are a number of open fifths, Holden's handling of harmonic materials is competent; there are no real dissonances, a minimum of parallel fifths and octaves, and the progressions sound "natural" to educated ears. There are even chromatic experiments such as those in measures 94 and 97.

Whether the paucity of contrapuntal texture reveals a deficiency in Holden's musicianship or a willful avoidance of textual entanglement, this is the one component of his style that is less than satisfactory.

Several characteristics are not illustrated in "The Lord is good to all." Holden is the only one of the New England anthem composers who deviated frequently from the standard four-part mixed choir. Of the twelve works, six are for three-part mixed chorus (treble, tenor, and bass). The consistent meter, too, is not wholly typical. In about half the pieces the meter and tempo change several times either at sectional divisions or within phrases. The strong element of abstract musical form (see the recurrent refrain at mm. 18, 45, 62, and 108) is not typical of Holden. Most of the anthems emphasize continuity rather than sectionalization, and there is rarely any repetition of musical materials.

Finally, Holden's mentor, direct or indirect, must be identified as Hans Gram, thanks to several mannerisms which, in combination, could hardly have been acquired elsewhere. One is his frequent use of the fermata (on both notes and rests) in all anthems from 1796 on; another is the occasional appearance of "sighing" figures in repeated suspensions; the last is the sudden introduction of a choral unison which often produces a dramatic effect such as that in Figure 36.

29. Holden, *Union Harmony*, p. xiii.

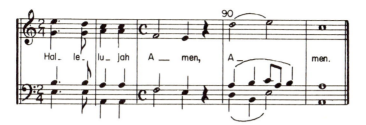

from: Holden, <u>Union Harmony</u>, 1793, Vol. II, p. 7.

FIG. 36. Holden, "Hear my cry, O God," mm. 87–91

JACOB KIMBALL

One year later than those of Holden, the first anthems of Jacob Kimball appeared in publication. Born in Topsfield, Massachusetts, in 1761, Kimball was the son of the local blacksmith who "set ye tunes" (i.e., lined out) in the Topsfield church. After service as a drummer in Little's Regiment of the Massachusetts militia during the Revolution, he graduated from Harvard College in 1780, studied law, and was admitted to the bar in Stratford, New Hampshire, in 1782. His fondness for music soon terminated his legal career, however, and he returned to Topsfield, where he began a lifetime occupation as a teacher of singing schools. Particularly regrettable in view of his promising youth, Kimball died, an alcoholic, in the almshouse in Topsfield on February 6, 1826.[30]

Kimball's five anthems first appeared in two of his collections of church music (see Table 8). A third collection, *The Essex Harmony, Part II*, was issued in 1803, but it contained no new anthems by the compiler. The popularity of "I heard a great voice from heaven," as indicated by the list of publications in Table 8, illustrates a new trend that originated during the last decade of the eighteenth century and flourished throughout the nineteenth century—the application of the designation "anthem" to a piece of congregational music. That work is Kimball's shortest (forty-eight measures) in form and is simpler in all aspects than many of the psalm and hymn tunes in the same collection. Repetition of words and phrases and a prose text seem to have been the only reasons for calling it an anthem rather than a hymn.

Kimball's anthems, as a whole, are very attractive pieces and are superior to many that were current at the time. For that reason, it is difficult

---

30. Metcalf, *op. cit.*, pp. 111–14.

to understand the basis for an attack directed at *The Essex Harmony* by the Reverend William Bentley of Salem. In a diary entry of late 1800, he wrote:

> Mr. McNulty has published a book of Kimball's psalmody. This young man was very amiable until he became addicted to intemperance. It is lamentable that so many publications in this country are evidently only catch-penny productions—not even suggested by genius but first asked by the promise of cash for the compilation.[31]

TABLE 8

PUBLICATION IN NEW ENGLAND OF ANTHEMS BY JACOB KIMBALL

Blessed is he who considereth the poor (6) *
I heard a great voice from heaven (1, 3, 4–5, 7–8)
O come sing unto the Lord (1, 2)
O Lord, Thou art my God (1)
They who put their trust in the Lord (6)

Date	Publication	Number of Anthems
1. 1793	Kimball, *Rural Harmony*	3
2. 1793	Holden, *Union Harmony*, Vol. II	1
3. 1801	The same, Vol. I, 3d ed.	1
4. 1798	*Village Harmony*, 4th ed.	1
5. 1800	The same, 5th ed.	1
6. 1800	Kimball, *Essex Harmony*	2
7. 1800	*Worcester Collection*, 7th ed.	1
8. 1803	The same, 8th ed.	1

* See note to Table 1 for an explanation of numbers in parentheses.

Since Kimball's style is almost identical with that of Holden, none of his works is included in the Musical Supplement. Holden's "The Lord is good to all" (in the Musical Supplement) is equally representative of both men. The differences in style are largely differences in degree rather than in kind; they lie in such relatively insignificant aspects as a greater incidence of Italian dynamic indications, fewer solo parts, and the absence of florid melismatic passages in Kimball's anthems.

Kimball's harmonic idiom differs slightly from Holden's, too, in that it revolves even more closely around the principal chords. There are many extended passages requiring only tonic and dominant triads. Within the

31. *Ibid.*, p. 113.

context of this meager harmonic vocabulary, however, there are likely to be fewer incomplete triads than in a Holden work, sometimes as few as 2 per cent of the chords. The greater sonority is especially apparent at cadences where complete authentic formulas (V-I or V_7-I) replace those involving an open fifth.

The benefits of Kimball's association with Hans Gram are evident, particularly in the two later works, where a choral unison and an effective use of dynamic contrast result in a more fervent expressiveness. The nature of their association is not clear. It could not have been very extensive, since Kimball was a resident of Topsfield whereas Gram lived either in Charlestown or in Boston, but Kimball's knowledge and approval of Gram's music is documented. He, along with N. Fay and Isaac Lane, endorsed Gram's *Sacred Lines for Thanksgiving Day* with a statement printed on the second page of that collection:

> We the subscribers have perused a manuscript copy of an ANTHEM and several PSALM TUNES, composed by Mr. Hans Gram, of Boston, and do readily and chearfully [*sic*] give it as our opinion, that the aforesaid Anthem and Tunes are so well composed, both as to Melody and Harmony, as to render them deserving of a favourable reception from every lover of sacred Music; and we do hereby recommend them to all schools and singing societies both in Town and Country, as suitable compositions to be used on a Thanksgiving Day, etc.

It may be that Gram, as an immigrant, felt the need of local sponsorship. At any rate, it was a gracious gesture on the part of three rival composers and indicates that they enjoyed sufficient recognition as musicians to make their endorsement significant.

Two further characteristic details of Kimball's style are illustrated in Figure 37 in the many repeated notes (see the melodic line in the tenor part) and the extreme simplicity, even rigidity, of the rhythmic scheme.

from: Kimball, Rural Harmony, 1793, p.50.

FIG. 37. Kimball, "O come sing unto the Lord," mm. 25–32

SUPPLY BELCHER

Supply Belcher was the only representative of the District of Maine among the anthem composers of the eighteenth century. In 1774 he was a member of William Billings' singing school in Stoughton, Massachusetts, where he was born on March 29, 1751, and where he was the proprietor of a tavern before moving to Maine in 1785. Belcher's Tavern seems to have been the social center of Stoughton's musical set, and he was a leader in all musical activities. After six years in Hallowell (now Augusta), Maine, he settled in Farmington in 1791, and remained there until his death on June 9, 1836.[32]

His very active life in Farmington is reminiscent of Oliver Holden's in Charlestown; in addition to his occupation as a teacher, he was a justice of the peace, town clerk and selectman, taught singing schools, directed the music in the local church, and was sometime representative of Farmington to the Massachusetts legislature before Maine became an independent state in 1820. His local prestige as a musician is revealed in a newspaper account of a concert in Hallowell in 1796. There Belcher is referred to as "the Handel of Maine."

The compliment was, unfortunately, more flattering than fitting if his four anthems were the basis of this musical evaluation. The first three, "Angels roll the rock away," "Farewell, a sad and long farewell," and "Make a joyful noise unto the Lord," appeared only in Belcher's single published collection, *The Harmony of Maine* (1794). The fourth, "Hail, Thou King of Saints," was published in two forms in 1797—as an independent publication called *Mr. Belcher's Celebrated Ordination Anthem* and as a part of *The Worcester Collection* (6th ed.).

The pieces are a strange mixture of styles. The first two are as short and simple as many hymn tunes, and both are settings of metric poetry. The occasional repetition of a word or phrase is the only justification for their designation as anthems. (Indicative of the ambiguity of that designation for Belcher is the fact that two of the compositions indexed as "anthems" in *The Harmony of Maine* are the tunes "Omega" and "Transmigration.") The other two works are anthems proper—longer settings of prose Scriptural passages with short solo parts and textural variety in several polyphonic insertions.

Although there is evidence of some improvement in the last anthem, all four of the pieces bear witness to Belcher's meager musical training. The

32. George T. Edwards, *Music and Musicians of Maine*, p. 22.

meters, rhythms, harmonic rhythms, and textual accents are not co-ordinated. The harmonic language is marred by many incomplete triads, by a small percentage of seventh chords and inversions, by a preponderance of ungrateful chord progressions involving secondary triads, and by too many unjustified dissonances. Polyphonic sections, in the six instances when they do occur, are fragmentary and primitive. There is not even any redeeming increase in expressiveness gained by emancipation from "correct" technical procedures. Only one unique, and seemingly original, effect is worthy of illustration: in the last chord of one of the pieces, Belcher eliminates the parts one by one in the manner of some modern organists who attempt to simulate, in small brick or frame churches, the acoustical properties of large stone cathedrals (see Fig. 38).

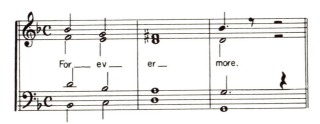

from: Belcher, Harmony of Maine, 1794, p.79.

Fig. 38. Belcher, "Farewell, a sad and long farewell," mm. 63–65

In 1795 two more "B"s—Babcock and Bull—made their first appearance as anthem composers.

Samuel Babcock

Samuel Babcock is known only through his one collection of church music, *The Middlesex Harmony* (1795; 2d ed., 1803). Two further facts may be gleaned from the prefaces of the two editions: first, that he was a resident of Watertown, Massachusetts, and, second, that his views regarding church music align him with the anti-Billings faction of composers. Writing in the third person, Babcock affirms that

> he has not consulted his own inclination entirely in introducing fuging music into pieces intended for public worship: But as it has been the general practice, wherever he has given in to it, he has endeavoured to preserve the sense of the lines entire, so as not to "make a jargon of the words." [33]

33. Babcock, *The Middlesex Harmony*, 2d ed., p. [ii].

Publication of Babcock's four anthems was confined to his own collection. "Comfort ye, my people," "Lord, Thou hast been our dwelling place," and "O come, let us sing unto the Lord" were included in both editions; "Remember now thy Creator" appeared for the first time in the second edition.

"O come, let us sing unto the Lord" (see Musical Supplement) contains all of the features that characterize Babcock's style. Only the melismatic figuration of the tenor part in the "Hallelujah" section and the final plagal cadence are not typical of the other three anthems. It is worthy of note, also, that the combination of the 2/4 metric signature with the tempo indication "Slow" at measure 66 is prophetic of the early nineteenth century when metric signatures lost their temporal significance.

Whoever he was, Babcock had managed to achieve a very adequate technique of composition by 1795, although the two polyphonic sections in "O come, let us sing unto the Lord" (mm. 16–21 and 84–88), where he was not able to maintain the imitation in the fourth entry, reveal that he was not a finished craftsman. But the satisfactory handling of metric, rhythmic, harmonic, and melodic materials produces a competent and attractive music, and, while there is nothing particularly distinctive or original about the anthems, they could be successfully performed today.

AMOS BULL

Amos Bull is another of those tantalizingly nebulous figures about whom almost nothing is known except for one publication. His birth date, 1744, is known only because of an advertisement in a New Haven newspaper of 1766 where Bull stated that he was twenty-two years old. The title page of his collection of church music and a newspaper advertisement dated July 5, 1805, establish his residence as Hartford, Connecticut. A reference to a Mr. Bull, singing master in New York, appeared in 1775 when Oliver King advertised for subscribers to his *Universal Harmony;* perhaps it was the same man.[34]

In the number of anthems published, Bull ranks with Holden, and second only to Billings. His twelve works in that form were published together in his collection, *The Responsary,* in 1795. There is a further distinctive unity in that the pieces are assigned numbers (e.g., "Anthem I. From the 104th Psalm," "Anthem II. From the 150th Psalm," etc.). In

---

34. Metcalf, *op. cit.,* p. 93.

alphabetical order, and with Bull's numbering indicated in parentheses, they are as follows:

> Arise, O Lord, into Thy resting place (IX)
> Arise, shine, O Zion (V)
> Behold, I bring you tidings (VIII)
> O be joyful in the Lord (IV)
> O Lord, revive Thy work (XII)
> O Lord, Thou art God (VII)
> O Lord, Thou hast searched me (X)
> O praise God in His holiness (II)
> O sing unto the Lord (VI)
> Ponder my words, O Lord (XI)
> Praise the Lord, O my soul (I)
> Thou art my portion, O Lord (III)

It is doubtful that Bull's numbers represent chronological order of composition; they seem to have been arbitrarily assigned on the basis of the order in which the anthems appear in the collection.

In view of the possibilities of such a large and homogeneous collection, Bull's anthems are a major disappointment. Some aspects of the harmonic idiom are even more inept than that of Billings' first attempts. In some of the pieces as many as 30 per cent of the sonorities are incomplete triads; the average incidence is between 20 and 25 per cent. And the low proportion of seventh chords (there are *none* in one of the pieces) and inversions emphasizes the primitive effect. Two distinctive features of the harmonic scheme are the numerous cadences upon a tonic unison, and the peculiar spacing of the parts on two distinctive planes, with the two upper parts often separated from the lower ones by an octave or more. The latter effect is a result of Bull's setting the whole collection for two trebles, tenor, and bass rather than for the usual treble, counter, tenor, and bass. He explains this deviation in a prefatory statement to the effect that

> Second Trebles are preferred to Counters, which are not adapted to women's voices; and which we can very seldom find men's voices sufficient for—and it has not been regarded which Treble ran highest, as it makes little or no difference in the musick.[35]

This same dualism of the women's and men's voices is a consistent textural factor in almost all of the pieces where antiphonal exchange between the two

35. Bull, *The Responsary*, p. 7.

levels is the usual means of introducing variety into the basic four-part chordal style. Minute polyphonic insertions, usually duet-style passages in non-imitative counterpoint, occur in only two of the twelve anthems. Another distinctive feature is the aimless character of the melodic lines. There is such melodic ambiguity, in fact, that it is often impossible to ascertain whether the first treble part or the tenor part is supposed to be the melody.

That nine of the anthems are settings of selected passages from the Prayer Book version of the Psalms (rather than the King James Version used by most composers) may be an indication that Bull designed his collection for Episcopal rather than Congregational churches.

Isaac Lane

In the same year that Babcock and Bull published their first anthems, the following advertisement appeared in the local newspapers on February 18, 1795:

> This Day Published . . . A Christmas Anthem. The Hymn Being in commemoration of the Birth of Our Divine Saviour, by Dr. Isaac Watts, and set to musick by Isaac Lane. Sold and Printed by Isaiah Thomas, jun., at his printing office, where subscribers will please to call for their copies.[36]

No copy of that rather unseasonable release seems to have survived, but the advertisement itself is valuable as one of the four extant documents relating to the composer.

The few facts known about the life of Isaac Lane have been derived almost solely from his publications. His residence was given as Bedford, Massachusetts, in the list of subscribers to Samuel Holyoke's *Harmonia Americana* in 1791, and he was one of the signers of the endorsement printed in Hans Gram's *Sacred Lines for Thanksgiving Day* in 1793. In 1797, two years after his first anthem was issued, Lane published *An Anthem: Suitable to be Performed at an Ordination or at the Dedication of a Meetinghouse*. As an independent publication, it probably did not have a very great circulation during the eighteenth century, but it seems to have become rather popular during the nineteenth century.

The anthem, Lane's only extant work in that form, is a simple setting in metric verse of a portion of Psalm 32 beginning "Where shall we go to seek and find a habitation for our God?" Despite the relatively high frequency of

---

36. *Massachusetts Spy* (Worcester), February 18, 1795.

open fifths, the technical aspects of the composition are satisfactory. There is
no attempt at polyphonic writing, but the prevailing chordal style is relieved
occasionally by solos for the trebles and the unique device illustrated in
Figure 39 where the parts drop out successively with a little melodic
flourish.

from: (Boston) First Church Collection, 1806, p. 115.

FIG. 39. Lane, "Where shall we go," mm. 30–38

The model for several other musical devices utilized by Lane is readily
found in the works of Hans Gram, whose collection Lane had inspected and
endorsed in 1793. A fermata, several choral unisons, and a fondness for
seventh chords with the third omitted are all devices common to both men
and appearing only in the music of composers whose association with Gram
can be established.

An interesting direction for performance practice is printed on the page
facing the first page of the music. There Lane indicates that both men and
women are to sing both the treble and tenor parts. This disposition of the two
parts in octaves emphasizes an ambiguity inherent in the two melodic lines.
In most anthems of the period the role of the treble part is unequivocally
secondary to that of the tenor, but in this work both the treble and tenor parts
are characterized by sufficient innate "tunefulness" so that it is impossible to
assign primacy to one or the other. In view of the promise shown in "Where
shall we go," it is regrettable that the other work is lost and that nothing is
heard of Lane after 1797.

ELIAS MANN

Elias Mann, whose first published anthem appeared in the same year as Lane's surviving work, was born in Weymouth, Massachusetts, in 1750. Nothing is known of his activities until about 1790 when several of his secular pieces were published in the *Massachusetts Magazine* with the notation that he was a resident of Worcester, Massachusetts. He is next heard of in 1796 when he and his wife joined the First Congregational Church in Northampton, Massachusetts. From there he issued his first volume of church music, *The Northampton Collection* in 1797 (2d ed., 1802). He may have remained in Northampton as a teacher of singing schools until his death on May 12, 1825.[37] George Hood gives the contradictory information that he died in Springfield, Massachusetts, on May 25, 1825, and says that he was an "industrious and enterprising carpenter" as well as a music teacher.[38] Mann's endorsement of Abijah Forbush's *The Psalmodist's Assistant* indicates that he was a resident of Roxbury in 1803. The facts that his second collection, *The Massachusetts Collection of Sacred Harmony*, was published in Boston in 1807 and that he was a member of the group who met in Boston in that same year to organize the Boston Musical Society (parent body of the Handel and Haydn Society) are further evidence that he had left Northampton.

Only one of Mann's two known anthems was published during the eighteenth century. "I was glad when they said unto me" was included in both editions of *The Northampton Collection;* the other, "Where shall we go to seek and find," appeared only in Walter Janes's *The Massachusetts Harmony* of 1803.

Hood's explanation that Mann's "means for acquiring a knowledge of composition were limited" is certainly verified by the rhythmic and harmonic difficulties as well as by the formal fragmentation of the earlier work. It is distinguished only by the occurrence of a chantlike, psalmodic passage reminiscent of those which Billings occasionally introduced. The second anthem, removed from the "hymn" category thanks only to some repetition of words and phrases in the setting of the text, shows some improvement in the manipulation of musical resources. Although it, too, is a simple, chordal setting, there is a greater utilization of choral color (e.g., choral unisons) and a naïve but charming little madrigalism when a sudden fermata is applied to the word "wait."

37. Metcalf, *op. cit.*, pp. 81–82.
38. *Musical Herald*, September, 1882, p. 229.

Two other composers introduced in published collections of 1797 are represented by only one anthem each.

DANIEL BELKNAP

Daniel Belknap was born in Framingham, Massachusetts, on February 9, 1771, the son of the famous Captain Jeremiah Belknap whose slave, Peter Salem, killed Major John Pitcairn, the commander of the British forces at Bunker Hill. After a common-school education in Framingham, Belknap became a farmer and mechanic, but taught singing schools as a side line all his life. His first class was in Framingham when he was but eighteen years old. He resided there until 1812 when he moved to Pawtucket, Rhode Island, where he died in 1815, "worthy of the respect that was always accorded him." [39]

Only one, *The Harmonist's Companion* (1797), of Belknap's four published collections of church music appeared before 1800. The other three were *The Evangelical Harmony* (1800), *The Middlesex Collection of Sacred Harmony* (1802), and *The Village Compilation of Sacred Music* (1806). A compilation of twenty-two secular tunes, *The Middlesex Songster*, was issued in 1809.

The one eighteenth-century collection contained the composer's only known anthem, "See from the dungeon of the dead." Like Mann's "Where shall we go to seek and find," the work is on the borderline between hymn and anthem. Belknap, aware of its dual nature, indicated in a footnote that the "Anthem may be performed in any Hymn, which contains 3, 6, 9, or 12 verses; by omitting the second part." [40] The "second part" is the only feature of the piece which might justify its designation as an anthem. It is a Scriptural passage in prose inserted between the first two verses of the hymn. Four-part "familiar style" is preserved even in this second section, and there is no repetition of words or phrases; the definition of "anthem" must therefore be stretched a bit in order to admit it to that category. The harmonic-tonal organization is adequate, but Belknap had difficulty in reconciling harmonic rhythms and meter. It is understandable that the work appeared only once.

TIMOTHY SWAN

The other composer whose anthem appeared in 1797 is Timothy Swan. Swan was born in Worcester, Massachusetts, on July 23, 1758. His entire

39. Metcalf, *op. cit.*, pp. 146–48.
40. Belknap, *The Harmonist's Companion*, p. 26.

musical training consisted of three weeks of singing school in Groton, where he had gone to live with a brother, about 1774, after the death of his father. During that same year he served for a short time as a fifer in the army in Cambridge. In the following year Swan was apprenticed to a brother-in-law who was a hatter in Northfield, Massachusetts. After three years in Northfield, he moved to Simsbury, Connecticut, in 1799, where he lived until his return to Northfield in 1807. Described by his neighbors as "poor, proud, and indolent" as a result of his habit of rising late after reading far into the night, he was in charge of the library there before his death on his eighty-fourth birthday in 1842.[41]

Swan's one attempt at publication of church music, *The New England Harmony* (1801), was a financial failure, but several of his hymn tunes (e.g., "China" and "Poland") were popular and were included in other publications throughout the nineteenth century. Some are still in use to-day.

"The voice of my beloved," the only anthem by Swan, was published only once during the eighteenth century—in Oliver Brownson's *New Collection of Sacred Harmony* of 1797. That collection is very crudely engraved, and some of the questionable places in the music may not have been the composer's fault, but such passages as the series of parallels in Figure 40 indicate that Swan's three weeks in singing school in Groton were not sufficient.

from: Brownson, <u>New Collection of Sacred Harmony</u>, 1797, p. 42.

FIG. 40. Swan, "The voice of my beloved," mm. 41–46

The piece is a miniature (about two minutes) setting of three two-line stanzas of a metric version of Song of Solomon, 2. The shortness of the text is, in itself, quite significant in its implication that the composer was not

41. Metcalf, *op. cit.*, p. 106.

occupied with musical declamation. On the contrary, because of the necessarily numerous repetitions of words and phrases, the purely musical aspects of the composition assume primary importance. As a result, the work is very attractive despite its several technical deficiencies.

Two final composers, who figure properly in the development of the anthem during the nineteenth century, are mentioned here because their earliest anthems appeared during the last decade of the eighteenth century.

SAMUEL HOLYOKE AND WILLIAM COOPER

Samuel Holyoke, a native of Boxford, Massachusetts, was born on October 15, 1762. He was the grandnephew of Edward Holyoke, one of the early presidents of Harvard College, and the son of the Reverend Elizur Holyoke, pastor of the Congregational church in Boxford for forty-seven years. After graduation from Harvard with the class of 1789, Holyoke devoted his life to teaching and composing music, chiefly in Massachusetts and New Hampshire. He died, unmarried, on February 7, 1820, in Concord, New Hampshire.[42]

Only two of Holyoke's twelve publications were issued before 1800: *Harmonia Americana* (1791), a collection of tunes and anthems, and the tune *Exeter: For Thanksgiving*, published independently in 1798. In addition, Holyoke worked with Oliver Holden and Hans Gram in the compilation of *The Massachusetts Compiler* in 1795. The two anthems contained in the *Harmonia Americana*, "Comfort ye, my people" and "Praise waiteth for Thee, O God," are Holyoke's only two eighteenth-century publications in that form.[43]

Nothing at all is known about William Cooper except for his three publications of church music between 1792 and 1804, and only an independent publication of *An Anthem: Designed for Thanksgiving Day* ("The Lord hath done great things for us"), published in Boston in 1792, appeared before 1800.

The music of both Holyoke and Cooper is similar to that of Oliver Holden and thus shows a considerable improvement over the technical standards of the first generation of New England composers. Although

42. *Ibid.*, pp. 114–20.

43. Five unpublished anthems of about the same period are in a manuscript collection of tunes and anthems by Holyoke in the Lowell Mason Collection at the Yale University Library.

nothing is recorded regarding the musical training of either man, both the style of the music and their geographical proximity suggest that they were strongly influenced by Hans Gram. It is possible that either one or both might have had some formal instruction in composition from Gram or some other European-trained musician, for even these first attempts at anthem composition prophesy the rapid refinement of church music in New England which was destined to be fulfilled during the first half of the nineteenth century.

Whatever their background, Holyoke and Cooper represent a new chapter in the history of the anthem in New England—a chapter not dominated by the ubiquitous shadows of Tans'ur, Knapp, Williams, and Stephenson. Both define clearly their attitude toward the type of music inaugurated by Billings and perpetuated by most of the other New England composers. In the Preface to *Harmonia Americana*, Holyoke explains why "fuguing pieces" were generally omitted from the collection:

> . . . the principal reason why few were inserted was the trifling effect produced by that sort of music; for the parts, falling in, one after another, each conveying a different idea, confound the sense, and render the performance a mere jargon of words.
> . . . the music requires a moderate movement . . . because sentiment and expression ought to be the principal guide in vocal music.[44]

And Cooper speaks, in the Preface to his collection of 1804, *Beauties of Church Music*, of his desire to "restore dignity to church music."

It is the appearance and the effects of this attitude which establish the turn of the nineteenth century as the end of an epoch in the history of the anthem in New England.

Perspective

The answers to most of the questions proposed in the Introduction have appeared at pertinent points in the preceding pages. A speculative reply must necessarily be given to the most difficult query: what generated the aesthetic impulse?

It is impossible to single out as indisputably primary any one of the many interwoven stimuli which motivate any artistic movement. In regard to church music in New England during the eighteenth century one can only point out the abatement of the rigors of pioneer days, the waning of

---

44. Holyoke, *Harmonia Americana*, p. 4.

theological controversy, and the stimulation of the religious revival of the mid-century as contributing factors. With the pattern of their society and economy established, the New Englanders could devote more attention and energy to the pursuit of such ornaments as the arts. And with the church persisting, to a larger degree than in any other English colony, as the focal point of their lives, this cultivation would inevitably be applied to the worship of their God.

The story of church music in New England during its first two centuries can be divided naturally into three phases. The first one hundred years was limited to psalmody and its decline. Then, from about 1720 until about 1760, the major activity centered on the amelioration of congregational music, with the attendant institution of "singing schools." Two further innovations of the same period were the admission of hymns and of instrumental accompaniments into worship services. Finally, during the last forty years of the eighteenth century, there occurred the remarkable expansion in both quantity and quality of church music, extensive publication, the first musical products of native New England composers, and the introduction of the more ambitious forms with which this study has been concerned.

Before the Revolution, and to a large extent afterward, the pattern of church music resembled closely that of the same social and religious classes in England. But, despite a strongly persistent impression to the contrary, it was no slavish or inferior mirroring of English practices. There was a considerable element of originality dictated by the requirements of existing conditions, and Sonneck recognized as early as the beginning of the present century

> that, if psalmody in America was crude and amateurish, it was not very much more so than in England as represented by Tans'ur, Williams, etc., that Billings was a character, a personality more than a pioneer, that his and the tendencies of his rivals and imitators were working with tremendous force for the good of the future of choral music,—in short that it is easier to ridicule the technical short-comings of these "singing teachers" than to give them credit for their actual musical abilities and to ascertain their real historical importance.[45]

It is to be expected that the first anthems known in New England were those by composers of the mother country that appeared in collections of music brought into the Colonies. Augmenting these relatively limited sources, English anthems were published in numerous American collections

45. Oscar Sonneck, *Early Concert Life in America*, pp. 310–11.

between 1760 and 1800. These imported anthems have a much greater significance than that inherent in their usefulness to eighteenth-century singers. Along with their accompanying psalm and hymn tunes, they were the immediate models for the first attempts at musical creation by native composers, and, consequently, must be recognized as the very foundation of American musical culture.

It is difficult to avoid the unjustified enthusiasm and uncritical sympathy for one's own subject occasionally displayed by authors of studies such as this one. After "living with" the music over a period of years, one is likely to become so absorbed by subtle suggestions of development and improvement that a parental sort of blindness to obvious faults and imperfections becomes a hazard. But an appraisal as objective as such spiritual proximity will permit discloses a wide diversity in musical accomplishment among our first generations of native composers. There can be no blanket plea for the resurrection and restoration to modern repertory of all eighteenth-century American anthems.

Some of the composers proved, by doing the "correct" thing in the handling of a given chord progression, for instance, that when they did the "incorrect" thing in the same composition they were doing it because they wanted it that way. But, even when we accept the music in the composer's own terms, as we must accept the "crudities" of much pre-Renaissance music and not according to any ex post facto standards, one must admit that some of those who published anthems were simply incompetent in musical technique.

The New England anthem composers of the late eighteenth century produced a mixed heritage, but, thanks to the music of Billings, French, Read, Kimball, Holyoke, Cooper, and, especially, of Oliver Holden, it is a heritage to be contemplated with pride.

APPENDIX I

Anthems by Non-American Composers Published in New England before 1800

Already see the daughters of the land   HANDEL
Arise, shine, O Zion   WILLIAMS
Awake up, my glory   WANLESS
Be Thou my judge, O Lord   ADAMS
The beauty of Israel is slain   ARNOLD
The beauty of Israel is slain   KNAPP
Behold He is my salvation   SELBY
Behold how good and joyful   BROWN
Behold I bring ye tidings   TANS'UR
Behold I bring you glad tidings   STEPHENSON
Blessed are they that are pure   TANS'UR
Blessed be the Lord God of Israel (the last chorus in Williams' "O Lord God of
    Israel," sometimes published independently)
Bring unto the Lord   KNAPP
By the rivers of Babylon   ASHWORTH
The first man was of the earth   GRAM
Give the king Thy judgments   KNAPP
God be merciful unto us   TANS'UR
Great is the Lord   EVERITT
Glory to God   HANDEL
Hallelujah, for the Lord God omnipotent reigneth   HANDEL
Hear my prayer, O Lord   STEPHENSON

Hear, O heavens, and give ear, O earth   KNAPP
I beheld and lo a great multitude   ARNOLD
I heard a great voice   KNAPP
I heard a voice from heaven   WILLIAMS
I said I will take heed   KNAPP
I was glad when they said unto me   TANS'UR
I was glad when they said unto me   WILLIAMS
I will love Thee, O Lord   TANS'UR
I will magnify Thee, my God and King   TANS'UR
I will magnify Thee, O God   KNAPP
I will sing unto the Lord   KNAPP
If the Lord Himself   WEST
Is there not an appointed time   KNAPP
Jehovah reigns, let all the earth rejoice   TUCKEY
Know ye not that there is a great man fall'n   ROGERSON
Let the bright Seraphim   HANDEL
Lift up your heads   WILLIAMS
The Lord is my light   ANONYMOUS
O be joyful in the Lord   SELBY
O be joyful in the Lord   TANS'UR
O clap your hands together   TANS'UR
O clap your hands together   WEST
O give ye thanks unto the Lord   TANS'UR
O Lord God of Israel   WILLIAMS
O Lord our Governour   WEST
O Lord Thou hast searched me out   KNAPP
O praise the Lord, all ye heathen   ANONYMOUS
O praise the Lord, all ye heathen   WILLIAMS
O praise the Lord, all ye nations   SELBY
O praise the Lord, O my soul   TANS'UR
O praise the Lord of heaven   TANS'UR
O praise the Lord with one consent   HANDEL
O sing unto the Lord   ARNOLD
O that mine eyes would melt   ANONYMOUS
O Zion that bringest good tidings   STEPHENSON
Praise the Lord, O my soul   STEPHENSON
Praise the Lord, ye servants   STEPHENSON
Praise ye the Lord   GRAM
Preserve me, O God   ADAMS
Rejoice in the Lord, O ye righteous   TANS'UR
Since by man came death   HANDEL
Sing, O ye heavens   STEPHENSON
Sing unto the Lord   WILLIAMS

Sing ye merrily unto God our strength   TANS'UR
Tell ye the daughters of Jerusalem   CLARK AND GREEN
They that go down to the sea   TANS'UR
They that put their trust in the Lord   ADAMS
Unto us a child is born   KNAPP
We have heard with our ears   ANONYMOUS
We'll sing to God with one accord   GRAM
When Israel came out of Egypt   TANS'UR
When the Lord turned again the captivity of Zion   ADAMS

APPENDIX II

Anthems by Native Composers Published in New England before 1800

And I saw a mighty angel   BILLINGS
Angels roll the rock away   BELCHER
Arise, O Lord, into Thy resting place   BULL
Arise, shine, O Zion   BULL
As the hart panteth   BILLINGS
As the hart panteth   HOLDEN
The beauty of Israel is slain   BILLINGS
Behold array'd in light   WOOD
Behold how good and how pleasant   LEE
Behold how good and joyful   BILLINGS
Behold I bring you tidings   BULL
Blessed is he that considereth the poor (I)   BILLINGS
Blessed is he that considereth the poor (II)   BILLINGS
Blessed is he who considereth the poor   KIMBALL
By the rivers of Watertown   BILLINGS
Comfort ye, my people   BABCOCK
Comfort ye, my people   HOLYOKE
Descend from heaven, celestial dove   FRENCH
Down steers the base [sic]   BILLINGS
Down steers the bass   READ
Except the Lord build   BILLINGS
Farewell, a sad and long farewell   BELCHER

God is the King   BILLINGS
Great is the Lord   HOLDEN
Hail, Thou King of Saints   BELCHER
Hark! from the tombs a doleful sound   FROST
Hark, hear you not   BILLINGS
Hark, you mortals, hear the trumpet   MORGAN
Hark! suddenly bursting o'er our heads   LEE
Have pity on me (part of Billings' "Samuel the Priest," sometimes published
  separately)
Hear my cry, O God   HOLDEN
Hear my prayer, O Lord, give ear   BILLINGS
Hear my prayer, O Lord, my God   BILLINGS
Hear, O heavens, and give ear, O earth   BILLINGS
Hear, O heavens, and give ear, O earth   FRENCH
Hear our prayer, O Lord   READ
The heavens declare the glory of God   BILLINGS
Holy, holy, holy, Lord God Almighty   BENHAM
How amiable are Thy tabernacles, O Lord   HOLDEN
I am come into my garden   BILLINGS
I am the Rose of Sharon   BILLINGS
I beheld and lo a great multitude   FRENCH
I charge ye, O ye daughters of Jerusalem   BILLINGS
I heard a great voice from heaven   BILLINGS
I heard a great voice from heaven   KIMBALL
I know that my Redeemer lives   READ
I love the Lord   BILLINGS
I was glad when they said unto me   MANN
I will love Thee, O Lord   BILLINGS
I will praise Thee, O Lord   HOLDEN
Is any afflicted let him pray   BILLINGS
It is better to go to the house of mourning   READ
Let every mortal ear attend   BILLINGS
Let the shrill trumpet's warlike voice   LYON
Lift up your eyes   BILLINGS
Lift up your heads, O ye gates   FRENCH
Listen, O isles, unto me   HOLDEN
The Lord descended from above   BILLINGS
The Lord hath done great things   COOPER
The Lord is good to all   HOLDEN
The Lord is King   BILLINGS
The Lord is ris'n indeed   BILLINGS
The Lord reigneth   HOLDEN
Lord, Thou hast been our dwelling place   BABCOCK

Make a joyful noise unto the Lord　BELCHER
Man that is born of woman　HOLDEN
Mourn, Phar'oh and Ahab prevail　BILLINGS
My friends, I am going　BILLINGS
My friends, I am going　FRENCH
Now after these things I saw another angel　FRENCH
O be joyful in the Lord　BULL
O be joyful in the Lord　READ
O clap your hands together　BILLINGS
O come let us sing unto the Lord　BABCOCK
O come sing unto the Lord　KIMBALL
O God, my heart is fixed　BILLINGS
O God, Thou hast been displeased　BILLINGS
O Lord, Thou art God from everlasting　BULL
O Lord, Thou art my God　KIMBALL
O Lord, revive Thy work　BULL
O Lord, Thou hast searched me　BULL
O praise God in His holiness　BULL
O praise God, praise Him in His holiness　BILLINGS
O praise the Lord, O my soul　READ
O praise the Lord of heaven　BILLINGS
O sing unto the Lord a new song　BULL
O sing unto the Lord and praise His name　FRENCH
O Thou that hearest prayer　HOLDEN
O Thou to whom all creatures bow　BILLINGS
Ponder my words, O Lord　BULL
Praise the Lord, O my soul　BULL
Praise waiteth for Thee, O God　HOLYOKE
Remember now thy Creator　BABCOCK
Righteous art Thou, O Lord　FRENCH
Samuel the priest gave up the ghost　BILLINGS
Sanctify a fast　BILLINGS
See from the dungeon of the dead　BELKNAP
Sing, O daughter of Zion　CARPENTER
Sing, O ye heavens　HOLDEN
Sing praises to the Lord　BILLINGS
Sing ye merrily unto God　BILLINGS
The Song of Songs is Solomon's　FRENCH
The sound of the harp ceaseth　HOLDEN
The States, O Lord　BILLINGS
They that go down to the sea　BILLINGS
They who put their trust in the Lord　KIMBALL
Thou art my portion, O Lord　BULL

Thou, O God, art praised in Sion   BILLINGS
Vital spark of heavenly flame   BILLINGS
The voice of my beloved   SWAN
Was not the day dark and gloomy   BILLINGS
We have heard with our ears   BILLINGS
When the Lord turn'd again the captivity   BILLINGS
Where shall we go to seek and find   LANE
Where shall we go to seek and find   MANN
Where shall we go to seek and find   WOOD
Who is this that cometh   BILLINGS
Why dost thou sit solitary   FRENCH

Bibliography

Books, Articles, and Manuscripts

Allen, William. *American Biographical Dictionary.* 3d ed. Boston: John P. Jewett & Co., 1857.

Barbour, J. Murray. *The Church Music of William Billings.* East Lansing: Michigan State University Press, 1960.

"Bio-Bibliographical Index of Musicians in the United States of America from Colonial Times." District of Columbia Historical Records Survey, Division of Community Service Programs, Works Projects Administration. Washington, D.C.: Music Division, Pan American Union, 1941 (mimeographed).

The Book of Common Prayer, and Administration of the Sacraments, and Other Rites and Ceremonies of the Church, According to the Use of The Church of England. London: John Baskett, 1727.

Brown, James D., and Stephen S. Stratton. *British Musical Biography.* Birmingham: S. S. Stratton, 1897.

Buechner, Alan C. "Yankee Singing Schools and the Golden Age of Choral Music in New England, 1760–1800." Ph.D. dissertation, Harvard University, 1959.

Bumpus, John S. *A History of English Cathedral Music, 1549–1889.* 2 vols. London: Laurie, [1908].

Chitwood, Oliver P. *A History of Colonial America.* New York: Harper & Bros., 1931.

Cotton, John. *Singing of Psalmes a Gospel Ordinance.* London: H. Allen, 1647.

Davey, Henry. *History of English Music.* London: J. Curwen & Sons, [1895].

Eames, Wilberforce. *List of Editions of the Bay Psalm Book.* New York, 1885.

EDWARDS, GEORGE T. *Music and Musicians of Maine*. Portland: Southworth Press, 1928.

EITNER, ROBERT. *Biographisch-bibliographisches Quellen-Lexikon der Musiker und Musikgeleherten*. Leipzig: Breitkopf & Haertel, 1900–1904.

ELLINWOOD, LEONARD. *The History of American Church Music*. New York: Morehouse-Gorham, 1953.

EVANS, CHARLES. *American Bibliography, 1639–1820* A.D. 12 vols. Chicago: Blake, 1903–34.

EVELYN, JOHN. *Diary*. 3 vols. Edited by Austin Dobson. London: Macmillan & Co., Ltd., 1906.

FELT, JOSEPH B. *History of Ipswich, Essex, and Hamilton*. Cambridge, Mass.: Folsom, 1834.

FOSTER, MYLES B. *Anthems and Anthem Composers*. London: Novello & Co., 1901.

GAGE, THOMAS. *The History of Rowley, anciently including Bradford, Boxford, and Georgetown*. Boston: Ferdinand Andrews, 1840.

[GILMAN, SAMUEL.] *Memoirs of a New England Village Choir*. Boston: S. G. Goodrich & Co., 1829.

GOULD, NATHANIEL D. *Church Music in America*. Boston: A. N. Johnson, 1853.

[HOLDEN, OLIVER. Incidents in the Life of Oliver Holden.] Manuscript letter to George Hood now in Music Department of the Boston Public Library. [Charlestown, 1842.]

HOOD, GEORGE. *A History of Music in New England*. Boston: Wilkins, Carter & Co., 1846.

HOWARD, JOHN TASKER. *Our American Music*. 3d ed. New York: Thomas Y. Crowell Co., 1946.

HUNT, WILLIAM. "England, Church of," *Encyclopaedia Britannica*, 11th ed. Vol. IX.

LIGHTWOOD, JAMES T. *Hymn-Tunes and Their Story*. London: C. H. Kelly, [1905].

LINCOLN, WILLIAM. *History of Worcester, Massachusetts, from Its Earliest Settlement to September, 1836*. Worcester: Phillips & Co., 1837.

LINDSTROM, C. "William Billings and His Time," *Musical Quarterly*, XXV (October, 1939), 479–97.

LOCKE, MATTHEW. *The Present Practice of Music Vindicated*. London, 1673.

LOWENS, IRVING. "Daniel Read's World: The Letters of an Early American Composer," *Notes of the Music Library Association*, ser. 2, IX (March, 1952), 233–48.

MACE, THOMAS. *Musick's Monument*. London: Ratcliff & Thompson, 1676.

Massachusetts Historical Society Collections, ser. 2, IV. Boston: Massachusetts Historical Society, 1816.

MATHER, INCREASE, et al. *A Letter; about the Present State of Christianity, among the Christianized Indians of New-England*. Boston: T. Green, 1705.

METCALF, FRANK J. *American Psalmody* . . . *1721–1820*. New York: C. F. Heartmann, 1917.

———. *American Writers and Compilers of Sacred Music.* New York: Abingdon Press, 1925.

PEPYS, SAMUEL. *Diary.* Edited by Henry B. Wheatley. 9 vols. London: G. Bell & Sons, Ltd., 1924–26.

POHL, C. F. *Mozart und Haydn in London.* Vienna: Carl Gerold's Sohn, 1867.

PRATT, WALDO SELDEN. *The Music of the Pilgrims.* Boston: O. Ditson Co., 1921.

SABIN, JOSEPH. *A Dictionary of Books Relating to America, from Its Discovery to the Present Time.* 29 vols. New York: J. Sabin, 1868–1936.

SACHS, CURT. *Rhythm and Tempo.* New York: W. W. Norton & Co., 1953.

SCHOLES, PERCY A. *The Puritans and Music; in England and New England.* London: Oxford University Press, H. Milford, 1934.

SEWALL, SAMUEL. "Diary," *Collections of the Massachusetts Historical Society,* ser. 5, Vol. III. Boston: The Society, 1882.

SONNECK, OSCAR G. T. *Early Concert Life in America, 1731–1800.* Leipzig: Breitkopf & Haertel, 1907.

———. *Francis Hopkinson, the First American Poet-Composer (1737–1791) and James Lyon, Patriot, Preacher, Psalmodist (1735–1794).* Washington, D.C.: Printed for the Author by H. L. McQueen, 1905.

[SYMMES, THOMAS.] *The Reasonableness of Regular Singing, or, Singing by Note.* Boston: B. Green for S. Gerrish, 1720.

WALKER, ERNEST. *A History of Music in England.* Oxford: At the Clarendon Press, 1907.

WARRINGTON, JAMES. *Short Titles of Books Relating to . . . the History . . . of Psalmody in the United States, 1620–1820.* Philadelphia: J. Warrington, 1898.

WINSLOW, EDWARD. *Hypocrisie Unmasked. A True Relation of the Proceedings of the Governor and Company of the Massachusetts against Samuel Gorton of Rhode Island.* London: J. Bellamy, 1646. Reprinted from the original edition by the Club for Colonial Reprints, Providence, R.I., 1916.

YOUNG, ALEXANDER. *Chronicles of the Pilgrim Fathers of the Colony of Plymouth, from 1602–1625.* Boston: Little and Brown, 1844.

MUSIC

The anthems contained in publications that first appeared in America are listed in this bibliography in alphabetical order according to the name of the composer and the first line of the text.

ADAMS, ABRAHAM. *The Psalmist's New Companion.* 11th ed. London: S. & P. Thompson [1803?].

AINSWORTH, HENRY. *The Book of Psalms.* Amsterdam: Giles Thorp, 1612.

American Musical Magazine. Vol. I. 12 monthly nos. New Haven: Doolittle and Read, 1786–87.

    ADAMS, Be Thou my judge, O Lord

    ADAMS, When the Lord turned again

    WANLESS, Awake up, my glory

ARNOLD, JOHN. *The Complete Psalmodist: or the Organist's, Parish-clerk's and Psalm-singer's Companion.* 7th ed. London: Buckland, Rivington, Crowder, Longman, and Law, 1779.

ARNOLD, SAMUEL. *Cathedral Music.* 2d ed. Edited by Edward F. Rimbault. London: Novello, 1846.

BABCOCK, SAMUEL. *The Middlesex Harmony.* Boston: Thomas & Andrews, 1795.

    BABCOCK, Comfort ye my people

    BABCOCK, Lord, Thou hast been our dwelling place

    BABCOCK, O come let us sing unto the Lord

———. *The Middlesex Harmony.* 2d ed. Boston: Thomas & Andrews, 1803. Same anthem content as in first edition with one additional anthem:

    BABCOCK, Remember now thy creator

The Bay Psalm Book. See *The Whole Booke of Psalmes.*

BAYLEY, DANIEL. *The New Harmony of Zion.* Newburyport: D. Bayley, 1788.

    CLARK and GREEN, Tell ye the daughters of Jerusalem

    STEPHENSON, Behold, I bring you glad tidings

———. *The New Universal Harmony, or Compendium of Church Music.* Newburyport: D. Bayley, 1773.

    ARNOLD, Great is the Lord

    ARNOLD, I beheld and lo a great multitude

    ASHWORTH, By the rivers of Babylon

    BROWN, Behold how good and joyful

    KNAPP, The beauty of Israel

    KNAPP, Bring unto the Lord

    KNAPP, Hear, O heavens, and give ear, O earth

    KNAPP, I heard a great voice from heaven

    KNAPP, I said I will take heed

    KNAPP, I will magnify Thee, O God

    KNAPP, I will sing unto the Lord

    KNAPP, Is there not an appointed time

    KNAPP, O Lord, Thou hast searched me out

    KNAPP, Unto us a Child is born

    STEPHENSON, Praise the Lord, O my soul

    WANLESS, Awake up, my glory

    WILLIAMS, Arise, shine, O Zion

WILLIAMS, The Lord is my light

WILLIAMS, O praise the Lord, all ye heathen

WILLIAMS, O that mine eyes would melt

BELCHER, SUPPLY. *The Harmony of Maine*. Boston: Thomas & Andrews, 1794.

BELCHER, Angels roll the rock away

BELCHER, Farewell, a sad and long farewell

BELCHER, Make a joyful noise unto the Lord

BELKNAP, DANIEL. *The Harmonist's Companion*. Boston: Thomas & Andrews, 1797.

BELKNAP, See from the dungeon of the dead

BENHAM, ASAHEL. *The Federal Harmony*. New Haven: Morse, 1790.

MORGAN, Hark! you mortals, hear the trumpet

———. *The Federal Harmony*. 2d ed. New Haven: Morse, 1792.

FRENCH, My friends I am going

MORGAN, Hark! you mortals, hear the trumpet

———. *The Federal Harmony*. 3d ed. Not located. Probably same anthem content as in 2d ed.

———. *The Federal Harmony*. 4th ed. Middletown: Woodward, [1794]. Same anthem content as 2d ed.

———. *The Federal Harmony*. 5th ed. Middletown: Woodward, [1795]. Same anthem content as 2d ed.

———. *The Federal Harmony*. 6th ed. Middletown: Woodward, [1796]. Same anthem content as 2d ed.

BENJAMIN, JONATHAN. *Harmonia Coelestis*. Northampton: A. Wright, 1799.

TUCKEY, Jehovah reigns, let all the earth rejoice

BILLINGS, WILLIAM. *An Anthem. Psalm 47. For Thanksgiving*. [Boston]: J. Norman, [*ca.* 1786].

———. *An Anthem. Psalm 127*. [Boston]: J. Norman, [*ca.* 1786].

———. *The Continental Harmony*. Boston: Thomas & Andrews, 1794. (All anthems by Billings.)

Hark! hear ye not

Hear, O heavens, and give ear, O earth

The heavens declare the glory of God

I am come into my garden

I charge ye, O ye daughters of Jerusalem

I will love Thee, O Lord

Mourn, Phar'oh and Ahab prevail

My friends, I am going

O God, my heart is fixed

O God, Thou hast been displeased

O praise God, praise Him in His holiness

O praise the Lord of heaven

O Thou, to whom all creatures bow

Sanctify a fast
Sing praises to the Lord
We have heard with our ears
When the Lord turned again
———. *Easter Anthem.* Boston: Thomas & Andrews, 1795.
———. *The New-England Psalm-Singer.* Boston: Eads & Gill, 1770. (All
anthems by Billings.)
As the hart panteth
Blessed is he that considereth the poor
Hear my prayer, O Lord
The Lord descended from above
The Lord is king
———. *Peace: an Anthem.* [Boston]: W. Billings, [*ca.* 1783].
———. *The Psalm-Singer's Amusement.* Boston: Billings, 1781. (All anthems
by Billings.)
And I saw a mighty angel
The beauty of Israel is slain
Blessed is he that considereth the poor
Down steers the base [*sic*]
Let every mortal ear attend
They that go down to the sea
Thou, O God, art praised in Zion
Vital spark of heavenly flame
Who is this that cometh
———. *The Psalm-Singer's Amusement.* 2d ed. n.p., [*ca.* 1805]. Same anthem
content as in 1st ed.
———. *The Singing Master's Assistant.* Boston: Draper & Folsom, 1778. (All
anthems by Billings.)
By the rivers of Watertown
Hear my prayer, O Lord my God
I am the Rose of Sharon
I heard a great voice from heaven
I love the Lord
Is any afflicted, let him pray
Sing ye merrily
The States, O Lord
Was not the day dark and gloomy
———. *The Singing Master's Assistant.* 2d ed. Boston: Draper & Folsom, 1779.
Same anthem content as 1st ed.
———. *The Singing Master's Assistant.* 3d ed. Boston: Draper & Folsom, 1781.
Same anthem content as 1st ed.
———. *The Singing Master's Assistant.* 4th ed. Boston: E. Russell, n.d. Same
anthem content as 1st ed.

BILLINGS, WILLIAM. *The Suffolk Harmony.* Boston: Printed by J. Norman for the Author, 1786. (All anthems by Billings.)
 Behold how good and how joyful
 Lift up your eyes
 The Lord is ris'n indeed
 Samuel the priest
 Bound in with copies in Houghton Library:
 Except the Lord build
 O clap your hands

BOYCE, WILLIAM. *Cathedral Music.* 3d ed. London: Novello, 1849.
———. *Services and Anthems.* 2d ed. 4 vols. London: V. Novello, 1846.

BROOME, MICHAEL (ed.). *A Choice Collection of Twenty-four Psalm Tunes.* Birmingham: [*ca.* 1738–40].

BROWNSON, OLIVER. *A New Collection of Sacred Harmony.* Simsbury, Connecticut: Brownson, [1797].
 BILLINGS, The Lord is ris'n indeed
 BILLINGS, Vital spark of heav'nly flame
 SWAN, The voice of my beloved

———. *Select Harmony.* [New Haven: T. and S. Green,] 1783.
In Boston Public Library copy I:
 BENHAM, Holy, Holy, Holy, Lord God Almighty
 KNAPP, Is there not an appointed time
 [WILLIAMS?], Arise, shine, O Zion
 ANON., O that mine eyes would melt
 ANON., We have heard with our ears

In Boston Public Library copy II:
 BENHAM, Holy, Holy, Holy, Lord God Almighty
 FRENCH, My friends, I am going
 KNAPP, Is there not an appointed time

In Library of Congress copy:
 BENHAM, Holy, Holy, Holy, Lord God Almighty
 KNAPP, Is there not an appointed time
 ANON., O that mine eyes would melt

BULL, AMOS. *The Responsary.* Worcester: I. Thomas, 1795. (All anthems by Bull.)
 Arise, O Lord, into Thy resting place
 Arise, shine, O Zion
 Behold, I bring you tidings
 O be joyful in the Lord
 O Lord, revive Thy work
 O Lord, Thou art God
 O Lord, Thou hast searched me

    O praise God in His holiness
    O sing unto the Lord
    Ponder my words, O Lord
    Praise the Lord, O my soul
    Thou art my portion, O Lord

CHENEY, SIMEON P. *The American Singing Book.* Boston: White, Smith & Co., 1879.

COOPER, WILLIAM. *An Anthem. Designed for Thanksgiving Day.* Boston: Thomas & Andrews, 1792.

The Federal Harmony. Boston: J. Norman, 178?.
    KNAPP, The beauty of Israel is slain
    KNAPP, I will sing unto the Lord
    WILLIAMS, Arise, shine, O Zion
    WILLIAMS, O Lord God of Israel

The Federal Harmony. [2d ed.?] Boston: J. Norman, 1790.
    WILLIAMS, Arise, shine, O Zion
    WILLIAMS, O Lord God of Israel
    SELBY, Behold, God is my salvation
    STEPHENSON, Behold I bring you glad tidings

The Federal Harmony. [3d ed.?] Boston: J. Norman, 1792.
    BENHAM, Holy, Holy, Holy, Lord God Almighty
    BILLINGS, The Lord is ris'n indeed
    SELBY, Behold, God is my salvation
    SELBY, O be joyful in the Lord

The Federal Harmony. [4th ed.?] Boston: J. Norman, 1793. Same anthem content as 1792 edition.

The Federal Harmony. 8th ed. Boston: William Norman, 1794.
    BILLINGS, The Lord is ris'n indeed
    SELBY, O be joyful in the Lord

FLAGG, JOSIAH. *A Collection of All Tans'ur's and a Number of Other Anthems from Williams, Knapp, Ashworth and Stephenson.* Boston: J. Flagg, [1766]. (Anthem content varies in different copies.)
    ASHWORTH, By the rivers of Babylon
    HANDEL, Already see the daughters
    KNAPP, The beauty of Israel
    KNAPP, Bring unto the Lord
    KNAPP, Give the king Thy judgments
    KNAPP, Unto us a Child is born
    STEPHENSON, Behold I bring you glad tidings
    STEPHENSON, O Zion that bringest glad tidings
    TANS'UR, Blessed are they that are pure
    TANS'UR, I will magnify Thee, O Lord
    TANS'UR, O be joyful in the Lord

TANS'UR, O clap your hands together
TANS'UR, O praise the Lord, O my soul
TANS'UR, O praise the Lord of heaven
TANS'UR, Rejoice in the Lord
TANS'UR, Sing ye merrily unto God
TANS'UR, They that go down to the sea
TANS'UR, When Israel came out of Egypt
WILLIAMS, I was glad when they said unto me
——. *A Collection of the Best Psalm Tunes . . . to Which Are Added Some Hymns and Anthems.* Boston: J. Flagg, 1764.
ANON., O praise the Lord, all ye heathen
TANS'UR, O give ye thanks unto the Lord
——. *Sixteen Anthems, Collected from Tans'ur, Williams, Knapp, Ashworth and Stephenson.* See Flagg, *A Collection of All Tans'ur's . . .*
FRENCH, JACOB. *The Harmony of Harmony.* Northampton: A. Wright, 1802.
ADAMS, Preserve me, O God
BILLINGS, Have pity on me, O ye my friends
BILLINGS, Who is this that cometh
FRENCH, Descend from heaven, celestial dove
FRENCH, Hear, O heavens, and give ear, O earth
FRENCH, Lift up your heads, O ye gates
FRENCH, O sing unto the Lord
——. *The New American Melody.* Boston: J. Norman, 1789. (All anthems by French.)
My friends, I am going
Now after these things
O sing unto the Lord
Righteous art Thou, O Lord
Why dost thou sit solitary
——. *The Psalmodist's Companion.* Worcester: I. Thomas, 1793.
BILLINGS, And I saw a mighty angel
FRENCH, My friends, I am going
FRENCH, The Song of Songs is Solomon's
HANDEL, Already see the daughters
GRAM, HANS. *The Massachusetts Compiler.* See entry under Oliver Holden.
——. *Resurrection. An Anthem for Easter Sunday.* Charlestown, 1794.
——. *Sacred Lines for Thanksgiving Day.* Boston: Thomas & Andrews, 1793.
GRAM, We'll sing to God with one accord
GRISWOLD, ELIJAH, and THOMAS SKINNER. *Connecticut Harmony.* [Hartford: *ca.* 1800]
CLARK, Tell ye the daughters
LEE, Behold how good and how pleasant

HOLDEN, OLIVER. *The American Harmony*. Boston: Thomas & Andrews, 1792. (All anthems by Holden.)
    The Lord is good to all
    The Lord reigneth
    O Thou that hearest prayer
    Sing, O ye heavens
————. *Occasional Pieces*. Boston: n.d.
    HOLDEN, As the hart panteth
    HOLDEN, Listen, O isles, unto me
————. *Plain Psalmody*. Boston: Thomas & Andrews, 1800.
    HOLDEN, Great is the Lord
————. *Sacred Dirges, Hymns, and Anthems, Commemorative of the Death of General George Washington*. Boston: Thomas & Andrews, [1800].
    HOLDEN, The sound of the harp ceaseth
————. *The Union Harmony*. 2 vols. in 1. Boston: Thomas & Andrews, 1793.

Vol. I:
    BILLINGS, The Lord is ris'n indeed
    HOLDEN, Man that is born of woman

Vol. II:
    BILLINGS, I heard a great voice
    HOLDEN, Hear my cry, O God
    KIMBALL, O come sing unto the Lord
    SELBY, Behold He is my salvation
    SELBY, O be joyful in the Lord
    STEPHENSON, Behold I bring you glad tidings
    STEPHENSON, Hear my prayer, O Lord
    STEPHENSON, O Zion that bringest good tidings
    STEPHENSON, Praise the Lord, O my soul
    STEPHENSON, Praise the Lord, ye servants
    WILLIAMS, Arise, shine, O Zion
    WILLIAMS, Blessed be the Lord God of Israel
    WILLIAMS, Lift up your heads, O ye gates
————. *The Union Harmony*. Vol. I. 2d ed. Boston: Thomas & Andrews, 1796. Same anthem content as 1st ed. with one additional:
    HOLDEN, How amiable are Thy tabernacles
————. *The Union Harmony*. Vol. I. 3d ed. Boston: Thomas & Andrews, 1801.
    HOLDEN, Man that is born of woman
    KIMBALL, I heard a great voice from heaven
————. OLIVER, HANS GRAM, and SAMUEL HOLYOKE. *The Massachusetts Compiler*. Boston: Thomas & Andrews, 1795.
    HANDEL, Let the bright Seraphim

HOLYOKE, SAMUEL. *Harmonia Americana*. Boston: Thomas & Andrews, 1791.
 HOLYOKE, Comfort ye, my people
 HOLYOKE, Praise waiteth for Thee, O God
———. *The Massachusetts Compiler*. See entry under Oliver Holden.
JANES, WALTER. *The Massachusetts Harmony*. Boston: Manning & Loring, 1803.
 JANES, Come let us sing a new made song
 MANN, Where shall we go to seek and find
JOCELYN, SIMEON. *The Chorister's Companion, Part III*. New Haven: Jocelyn & Doolittle, 1782.
 ARNOLD, Great is the Lord
 BILLINGS, Vital spark of heavenly flame
 TANS'UR, O be joyful in the Lord
———. *The Chorister's Companion*. 2d ed. New Haven: Jocelyn & Doolittle, 1788.
 ADAMS, Preserve me, O God
 BILLINGS, I am the Rose of Sharon
 BILLINGS, Vital spark of heavenly flame
 CLARK and GREEN, Tell ye the daughters of Jerusalem
 TANS'UR, O clap your hands together
 WILLIAMS, I heard a voice from heaven
 WILLIAMS, I was glad when they said unto me
KIMBALL, JACOB, JR. *The Essex Harmony*. Exeter, N.H.: H. Ranlet, 1800.
 KIMBALL, Blessed is he that considereth the poor
 KIMBALL, They who put their trust in the Lord
———. *The Rural Harmony*. Boston: Thomas & Andrews, 1793.
 KIMBALL, I heard a great voice from heaven
 KIMBALL, O come sing unto the Lord
 KIMBALL, O Lord, Thou art my God
———, *et al. The Essex Harmony, Part II*. Salem: Cushing, 1802.
 ANON., O praise the Lord, all ye heathen
 WANLESS, Awake up my glory
KNAPP, WILLIAM. *The New Church Melody*. 4th ed. London: Baldwin, 1761.
LANE, ISAAC. *An Anthem: Suitable to be performed at an Ordination or at the Dedication of a Meetinghouse*. Northampton: D. Wright & Co., 1797.
LANGDON, CHAUNCEY. *The Beauties of Psalmody*. New Haven: D. Bowen, 1786.
 BILLINGS, I heard a great voice from heaven
 BILLINGS, Vital spark of heav'nly flame
 CARPENTER, Sing, O daughter of Zion
LAW, ANDREW. *A Collection of the Best and Most Approved Tunes and Anthems*. See Law, *Select Harmony*.
———. *Select Harmony*. New Haven: T. and S. Green, [1778].

ARNOLD, The beauty of Israel
ARNOLD, O sing unto the Lord
ASHWORTH, By the rivers of Babylon
KNAPP, I said I will take heed
KNAPP, Is there not an appointed time
STEPHENSON, Behold I bring you glad tidings
STEPHENSON, Praise the Lord, O my soul
STEPHENSON, Sing, O ye heavens
WEST, If the Lord Himself
WEST, O clap your hands together
WEST, O Lord, our Governour
WILLIAMS, Arise, shine, O Zion
WILLIAMS, O Lord God of Israel

———. *Select Harmony*. 2d ed. New Haven: T. and S. Green, 1779. Same anthem content as 1st ed.

LYON, JAMES. *Urania*. Philadelphia: W. Bradford, 1761.

MANN, ELIAS. *The Northampton Collection of Sacred Harmony*. Northampton: D. Wright & Co., 1797.

BILLINGS, The Lord is ris'n indeed
MANN, I was glad when they said unto me.

———. *The Northampton Collection of Sacred Harmony*. 2d ed. Northampton: Wright, 1802. Same anthem content as first edition with one added:

KIMBALL, O come sing unto the Lord

The Massachusetts Harmony. Boston: J. Norman, [1784].

KNAPP, The beauty of Israel is slain
KNAPP, I will sing unto the Lord
WILLIAMS, Arise, shine, O Zion
WILLIAMS, Lift up your heads, O ye gates
WILLIAMS, O Lord God of Israel

The Massachusetts Harmony. 2d ed. Boston: J. Norman, [1785]. Same anthem content as 1st ed.

MORGAN, JUSTIN. *Judgment Anthem*. Dedham: H. Mann, 1810.

PILSBURY, AMOS. *The United States Sacred Harmony*. Boston: Thomas & Andrews, 1799.

ADAMS, When the Lord turned again
WILLIAMS, Lift up your heads, O ye gates

PLAYFORD, HENRY. *Harmonia Sacra*. London: E. Jones for H. Playford, 1688–93.

PLAYFORD, JOHN. *The Whole Book of Psalms*. London: W. Godbid for the Company of Stationers, 1677.

RAVENSCROFT, THOMAS. *The Whole Booke of Psalmes*. London, 1621.

READ, DANIEL. *American Musical Magazine*. See title entry.

———. *The American Singing Book*. New Haven: D. Read, 1785. Anthem content same in all editions: 2d, 1786; 3d, 1792; 4th, 1793; 5th, 1795; 6th, 1796.

    READ, Down steers the bass

    READ, O praise the Lord, O my soul

READ, DANIEL. *The Columbian Harmonist, Number II*. New Haven: D. Read, 1795.

    BILLINGS, The Lord is Ris'n

————. *The Columbian Harmonist, Number III*. New Haven: D. Read, 1795.

    BILLINGS, And I saw a mighty angel

    BILLINGS, I heard a great voice

    HANDEL, Since by man came death

    HANDEL(-READ), There were shepherds abiding; Glory to God

    READ, Hear our prayer, O Lord our God

    READ, I know that my Redeemer lives

    READ, It is better to go to the house of mourning

    READ, O be joyful in the Lord

Sacred Harmony. Boston: Daniel Willard & Thomas Lee, Jr., 1790.

    LEE, Behold how good and pleasant it is

    [LEE], Hark! suddenly bursting o'er our heads

SELBY, WILLIAM. *Two Anthems for Three and Four Voices*. Boston: Selby, 1782.

    SELBY, O be joyful in the Lord

    SELBY, O praise the Lord, all ye nations

Sixteen Anthems Collected from Tans'ur, Williams, Knapp, Ashworth and Stephenson. See entry under Flagg.

STERNHOLD, THOMAS, and JOHN HOPKINS. *The Whole Book of Psalms*. London: Printed by A. G. for the Company of Stationers, 1635.

STICKNEY, JOHN. *The Gentleman and Lady's Musical Companion*. Newburyport: D. Bayley, 1774.

    ADAMS, They that put their trust in the Lord

    ASHWORTH, By the rivers of Babylon

    CLARK and GREEN, Tell ye the daughters of Jerusalem

    KNAPP, Give the king Thy judgments

    KNAPP, I said I will take heed

    KNAPP, Is there not an appointed time

    LYON, Let the shrill trumpet's warlike voice

    STEPHENSON, Behold I bring you glad tidings

    STEPHENSON, O Zion that bringest good tidings

    STEPHENSON, Praise the Lord, O my soul

    STEPHENSON, Sing, O ye heavens

    TANS'UR, Behold I bring ye tidings

    TANS'UR, Blessed are they that are pure

    TANS'UR, God be merciful

    TANS'UR, I was glad when they said unto me

TANS'UR, I will magnify Thee, O Lord
TANS'UR, O clap your hands together
TANS'UR, O give ye thanks
TANS'UR, O praise the Lord, O my soul
TANS'UR, O praise the Lord of heaven
TANS'UR, Rejoice in the Lord, O ye righteous
TANS'UR, They that go down to the sea
TUCKEY, Jehovah reigns, let all the earth rejoice
WILLIAMS, Arise, shine, O Zion
WILLIAMS, Hark, what news the angels bring
WILLIAMS, I heard a voice from heaven
WILLIAMS, I was glad when they said unto me
WILLIAMS, Sing unto the Lord

STONE, JOSEPH, and ABRAHAM WOOD. *The Columbian Harmony.* Boston: Thomas & Andrews, 1793.
WOOD, Where shall we go to seek and find

TANS'UR, WILLIAM. *The Royal Melody Complete, or the New Harmony of Zion.* 3d ed. Boston: W. M'Alpine, 1767.
KNAPP, Give the king Thy judgments
All by Tans'ur:
Behold I bring ye tidings
Blessed are they that are pure
God be merciful unto us
I was glad when they said unto me
I will love Thee, O Lord
I will magnify Thee, my God
O clap your hands together
O give ye thanks
O praise the Lord, O my soul
O praise the Lord of heaven
Praise the Lord, O my soul
Rejoice in the Lord
Sing ye merrily unto God
They that go down to the sea
When Israel came out of Egypt

———. *The Royal Melody Complete or the New Harmony of Zion.* 4th ed. Newburyport: D. Bayley, 1768. Same anthem content as in 3d ed.

———. *The American Harmony, Vol. I, or Royal Melody Complete.* 5th ed. (Title changed with fifth edition, and combined with Aaron Williams' *Universal Psalmodist.*) Newburyport: D. Bayley, 1769. Same anthem content as in 3d ed.

———. *The American Harmony; or, Royal Melody Complete.* 6th ed. Newburyport: D. Bayley, 1771. Same athem content as in 3d ed.

TANS'UR, WILLIAM. *The American Harmony; or, Royal Melody Complete.* 7th ed. Newburyport: D. Bayley, 1771. Same anthem content as in 3d ed.

———. *The American Harmony; or, Royal Melody Complete.* 8th ed. Newburyport: D. Bayley, 1773. Same anthem content as in 3d ed.

———. *The American Harmony; or, Royal Melody Complete.* 9th ed. Newburyport: D. Bayley, 1774. Same anthem content as in 3d ed.

TUFTS, JOHN. *An Introduction to the Singing of Psalm Tunes.* 5th ed. Boston: S. Gerrish, 1726.

TURNER, JAMES, [compiler?]. *Tunes.* Boston: Jas. A. Turner, 1752.

The Village Harmony. 2d ed. Exeter: H. Ranlet, 1796.

    FRENCH, My friends, I am going

    KIMBALL, I heard a great voice from heaven

    WILLIAMS, Lift up your heads, O ye gates

The Village Harmony. 4th ed. Exeter: H. Ranlet, 1798. Same anthem content as in 2d ed.

WALTER, THOMAS. *The Grounds and Rules of Musick Explained.* Boston: Printed by J. Franklin for S. Gerrish, 1721.

———. *The Grounds and Rules of Musick Explained.* 6th ed. Boston: T. Johnson, 1764.

    KNAPP, The beauty of Israel

The Whole Booke of Psalmes. Cambridge [Massachusetts]: S. Day, 1640.

WILLIAMS, AARON. *The American Harmony, or Universal Psalmodist.* 5th ed. Newburyport: D. Bayley, 1769.

    CLARK and GREEN, Tell ye the daughters of Jerusalem

    LYON, Let the shrill trumpet's warlike voice

    STEPHENSON, Behold I bring you glad tidings

    STEPHENSON, O Zion that bringest good tidings

    TANS'UR, O be joyful in the Lord

    WILLIAMS, Hark! what news the angel brings

    WILLIAMS, I heard a voice from heaven

    WILLIAMS, I was glad when they said unto me

    WILLIAMS, Sing unto the Lord

———. *The American Harmony, or Universal Psalmodist.* 6th ed. Newburyport: D. Bayley, 1771. Same anthem content as in 5th ed.

———. *The American Harmony, or Universal Psalmodist.* 7th ed. Newburyport: D. Bayley, 1771. Same anthem content as in 5th ed.

———. *The American Harmony, or Universal Psalmodist.* 8th ed. Newburyport: D. Bayley, 1773. Same anthem content as in 5th ed.

———. *The American Harmony, or Universal Psalmodist.* 9th ed. Newburyport: D. Bayley, 1774. Same anthem content as in 5th ed.

———. *The Universal Psalmodist.* London: J. Johnson, 1763.

———. *Williams' New Universal Psalmodist.* 5th ed. London: J. Johnson, 1770.

WOOD, ABRAHAM. *A Hymn on Peace*. Worcester: A. Wood, 1784.

The Worcester Collection of Sacred Harmony. Worcester: I. Thomas, 1786.

    ARNOLD, The beauty of Israel

    CLARK and GREEN, Tell ye the daughters of Jerusalem

    FRENCH, I beheld and lo

    FROST, Hark from the tombs

    HANDEL, O praise the Lord with one consent

    HANDEL, Hallelujah, for the Lord God Omnipotent reigneth

    STEPHENSON, Behold I bring you glad tidings

    STEPHENSON, Praise the Lord, O my soul

    SELBY, Behold He is my salvation

    WEST, If the Lord Himself

    WEST, O Lord, our Governour

    WILLIAMS, Arise, shine, O Zion

    WILLIAMS, Lift up your heads, O ye gates

    WILLIAMS, O Lord God of Israel

The Worcester Collection of Sacred Harmony. 3d ed. Worcester: I. Thomas, 1791.

    FROST, Hark from the tombs

    WILLIAMS, Blessed be the Lord God of Israel

The Worcester Collection of Sacred Harmony. 5th ed. Worcester: I. Thomas, 1794.

    BILLINGS, The Lord is ris'n indeed

    GRAM, Praise ye the Lord

The Worcester Collection of Sacred Harmony. 6th ed., altered, corrected and revised, with additions, by Oliver Holden. Boston: Thomas & Andrews, 1797.

    BELCHER, Hail Thou King of Saints

    BILLINGS, The Lord is ris'n indeed

    HOLDEN, I will praise Thee, O Lord

    HOLDEN, Man that is born of woman

The Worcester Collection of Sacred Harmony. 7th ed. Boston: Thomas & Andrews, 1800.

    BILLINGS, The Lord is ris'n indeed

    KIMBALL, I heard a great voice from heaven

    HOLDEN, Man that is born of woman

The Worcester Collection of Sacred Harmony. 8th ed. Boston: Thomas & Andrews, 1803.

    BILLINGS, The Lord is ris'n indeed

    COOPER, The Lord hath done great things for us

Musical Supplement

An Anthem. Psalm XLVII

William Tans'ur

from: Flagg, Sixteen Anthems, 1766, pp. 41-42.

An Anthem. II Sam., 1ˢᵗ Chap.

William Knapp

The beau_ ty of Is_ r'el is slain up_ on thy high pla_ ces:

how are the migh_ ty, migh_ ty fall'n! How are the migh_ ty fall'n!

The beau _ ty of Is_ r'el is slain up_ on thy high pla_ ces.

(Repeat meas. 7–13)

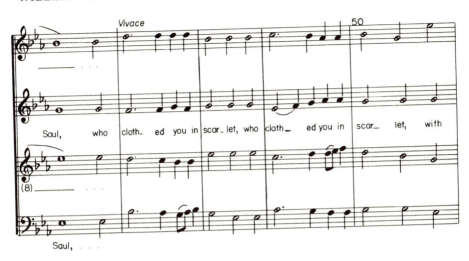

Saul, who cloth‿ed you in scar‿let, who cloth‿ed you in scar‿let, with

Saul, ...

o‿ther de‿lights. How are the migh‿ty, migh‿ty fall'n in the

midst_____ of the|bat_ tle! O Jon_a_than,thou| wast slain

O Jon_a_than, thou wast slain ____

in thine high |pla_ ces, thou wast slain in thine high pla_ ces. pla_ces.

Here sing the strain again: "Tell it not in Gath" (mm 20-26)

Tenor or Treble Solo

I am dis_tress_ed for thee, my bro_ther Jon_a_than. ve_ry pleas.ant hast thou been un_to me:

Bass Solo

thy love to me was won_der_ful, thy love to me was won_der_ful, pas_sing the love of wo_men.

Chorus Piano

How are the migh_ty, migh_ty fall'n, and the weap_ons of

(8)

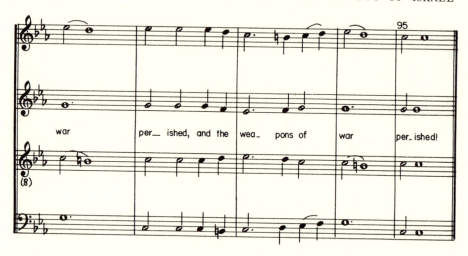

war   per— ished, and the wea— pons of   war   per— ished!

from: Walter, Grounds and Rules, 1764, pp. 37-41.

An Anthem, Psalm 122

Aaron Williams

(Tenor)

I was glad, was glad _____

I was glad, was . . .

was glad   when they said   un_to me   we will go,   we will go,

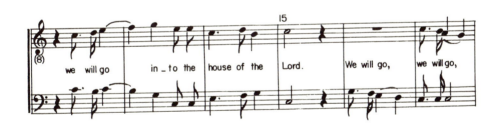

we will go   in_to the house of the   Lord.   We will go,   we will go,

we will go   in_ to the house of the   Lord.

Our   feet shall

our   feet shall   stand   in   thy gates, o._____

stand,   our . . .

Je _ ru_sa_lem . . .

Je _ ru_sa_lem is built   as   a   ci_ty that is at

Je _ ru_   sa_ lem.   Je _ ru_sa_lem . . .

u _ ni_ ty   in it_self,   for thi_ ther go   the tribes, the   tribes e_

for thi_ ther go   the   tribes . . .

for thi_ ther go, for thi_ ther go   the   tribes . . .

ven the tribes of the Lord, To tes_ti_fie un_to Is_ra_el, to tes_ti_fie

un_to Is_ra_el.

And to give

And to give thanks.

And to give thanks,

give

And to give thanks,

give thanks, give

thanks   un‗ to . . .

(8)   give   thanks un‗ to   the   name of the   Lord.   Lord.

(8)   thanks,   give   thanks un‗ to . . .

thanks   un‗ to . . .

Counter Solo   *tr*   *Tenor & Bass*

(8)   For   there is the seat of   judge‗   ment.   E‗ ven the   seat,

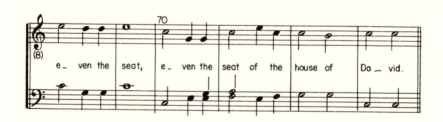

(8)   e‗ ven the seat,   e‗ ven the seat   of   the   house of   Da ‗ vid.

Chorus

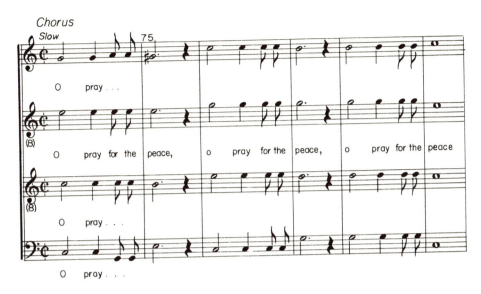

be with_in thy walls, peace be with_in thy walls, peace

be with_in thy walls, and plen_teous_ness,and plen_teous_ness with_in thy pa_ la_ces.

Counter 8 Bass

For my breth_ren and com_pan_ions' sakes

For my breth_ren and com_pan_ions' sakes   I will   wish thee pros_

I will   wish thee pros_per_i_ty,   I will wish thee pros_per_i_ty.

per_i_ty,   I will . . . .

For my   breth_ren and com_pan_ions'   sakes   I will wish thee pros_per_i_ty,   I   will

wish thee pros_ per_i_ty   and I will seek   to do thee   good.   good.

✻ N.B. Repeat "O pray... etc." and end with "Amen" Chorus

Chorus
Grave   Brisk

A_ men,   A_ men,   A_ men,   A_ men. Hal_le_lu_jah, hal_le_lu_jah,

from: Williams, <u>American Harmony</u>,

1771, pp. 43-47.

An Anthem out of the 2nd Chap. of Luke

Joseph Stephenson

Be _ hold I bring you glad tid _ ings, glad tid _ ings of joy which shall

be to all peo _ ple.

Be _ hold bring you glad tid _ ings, glad tid _ ings of

joy   which shall be   to   all   peo _ ple.   peo _ ple _

For   un _ to   you,   un _ to

you, un_to you is   born   this   day   in the ci _ ty of   Da_vid, in the ci _ ty of

you   is   born   this   day   in the ci _ ty,   in the ci _ ty of

David, a sav___iour which is Christ the Lord, a

sav___iour which is Christ the Lord.

Glad _____

God in the high-est, and on earth peace, peace good will to-wards men.

Hal-le-lu-jah ...

Hal-le-lu-jah, hal-le-lu-jah, hal-le-lu-jah,

Hal-le-lu-jah, hal-le-lu-jah, hal-le-lu-jah ...

Hal-le-lu-jah ...

from: Flagg, Sixteen Anthems, 1766, pp. 67-70.

Anthem   Psalm 8ᵗʰ

Benjamin West

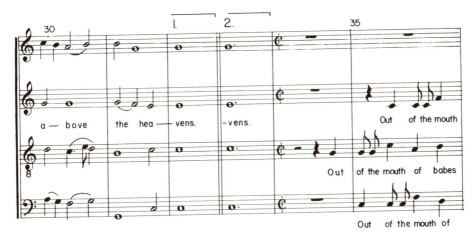

en ———————————————————— e- my   and the a- ven—ger.

I will con-si- der the hea_ vens, I will con-si- der the   heavens the

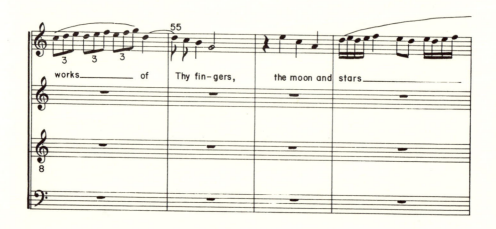

works—————— of Thy fin-gers,   the moon and stars—————

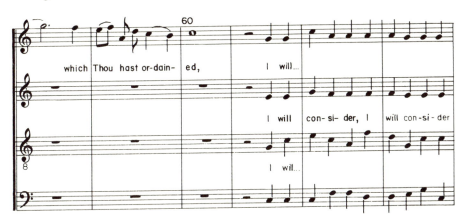

which Thou hast or-dain- ed, I will...

I will con-si- der, I will con-si-der

I will...

the hea-vens the works of Thy fin- gers.

What is man, what

What is man

What is man, what is

What is man, what is man, that Thou art mind-ful of him, that Thou art

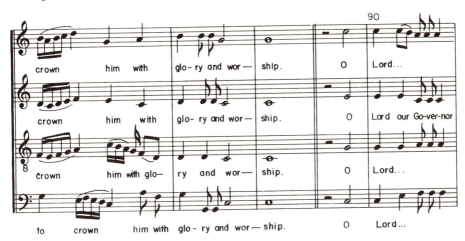

crown him with glo- ry and wor — ship. O Lord...

crown him with glo- ry and wor — ship. O Lord our Go-ver-nor

crown him with glo— ry and wor— ship. O Lord...

to crown him with glo- ry and wor—ship. O Lord...

how ex— cel—lent is Thy name in all the world.

Thanksgiving Anthem

William Selby

gates with thanks-giv——ing, with thanks-giv—ing, and in—to His courts with

praise,   be thank——ful un————to

be thank——ful un——-to Him, be...

Him, and speak, speak good of His name.   For the Lord is

LIVELY

gra-cious, for the Lord is gra-cious, and His mer-cy is e-ver-last—ing,

and His mer-cy

is ...

e—ver—last-ing,   e—ver—last—ing,   e—ver—last-ing, e—ver—

and His mer—cy   is...

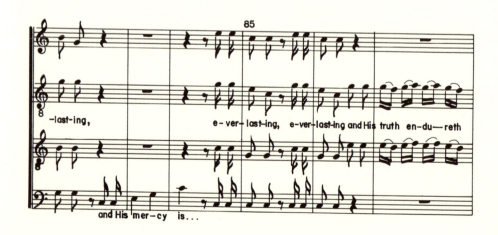

—last-ing,   e—ver— last-ing, e—ver—last-ing and His truth en—du——reth

and His mer—cy is...

from ge-ne-ra-tion to ge-ne—ra——tion, and His truth en-

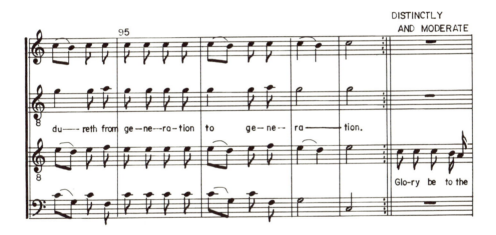

DISTINCTLY
AND MODERATE

du——reth from ge—ne—ra-tion to ge-ne—-ra——tion.

Glo-ry be to the

LIVELY

Glo—ry be to the Fa-ther, and to the

Fa-ther, and to the Son, and to the Ho—ly Ghost, . . .

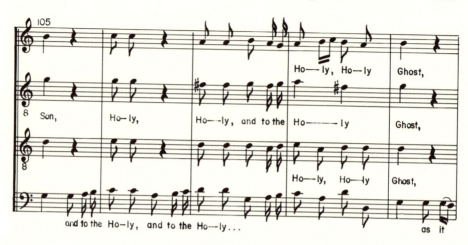

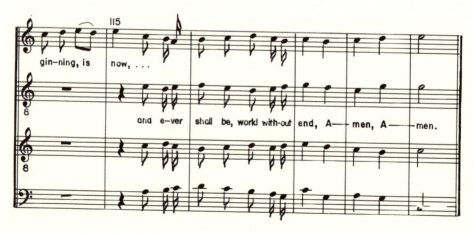

An Occasional Anthem

Hans Gram

God be on their mouth, and a two-edged sword in their hand, to ex-e-cute the judge-ment

ANDANTE STACATO
Tutti basso voces.

writ—ten: Bind kings with chains, bind kings with chains and no—bels with fet—ters of

i—ron, bind kings with chains, and no—bels with fet—ters of i—ron.

An Anthem. Psalm 42

William Billings

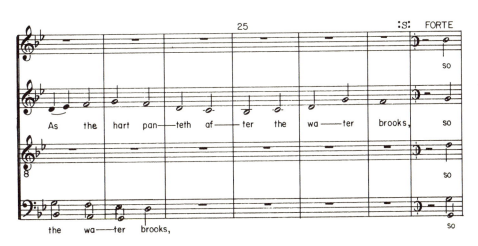

pan-teth...

pan-teth my   soul af—ter   Thee, O   God, so   pan-teth my   soul af—ter

S

Thee, O   God.

My   soul   thirs—teth

Dux

My   soul   thirs—teth for   the   Lord,   for the li—ving, for the li—ving

Trio

My   soul   thirs—teth   for   the   Lord,

for   the   Lord,   for the li—ving,   for the li—ving   God:

God_____: when   shall   I   come   and ap—pear be——fore   God __

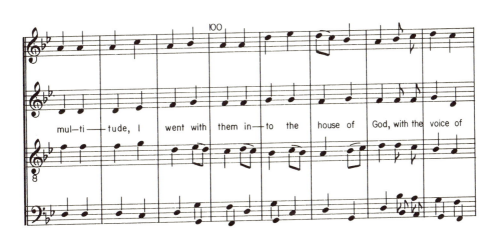

with a mul—ti————tude that keep ho——ly——day.

Sharp key

Why art thou cast down, O my soul? and why art thou dis—qui—et—ed with—in me?

Hope thou in God: for I shall yet praise Him for the help of His coun—te——nance.

ADAGIO
(Tenor)

O my God, my soul is cast down with in me:

there————fore will I re—mem—ber Thee from

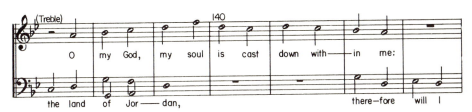

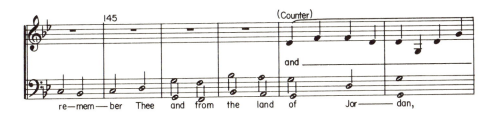

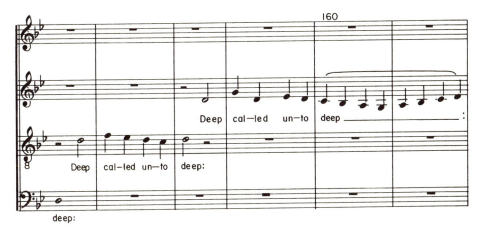

all thy waves   and thy bil—lows   are gone o—ver   me,   all   thy waves

and thy bil—lows   are gone o——ver   me.   Why   art   thou cast down,

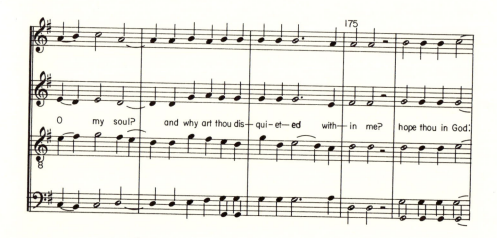

O   my soul?   and why art thou dis—qui—et—ed   with—in me?   hope thou in God:

for I shall yet praise Him for the help of His coun—te——nance.

Hal—le——lu—jah, Hal—le—lu—jah,

Hal—le——lu—jah, Hal—le—lu—jah,

Hal——le—lu—jah, Hal—le—lu—jah, Hal—le—lu—jah, Hal—

Hal——le————lu—jah, Hal—le—lu—jah,

A—men, Hal—le—lu—jah, A—men, A—men.

A—men, Hal—le—lu—jah, A—men, A—men.

—le—lu—jah, Hal——le—lu—jah, Hal—le——lu—jah.

A—men, Hal—le—lu—jah, A—men, A—men.

Sing the last strain (m.m. 190-201) three times.

An Anthem, Psalm 116th

William Billings

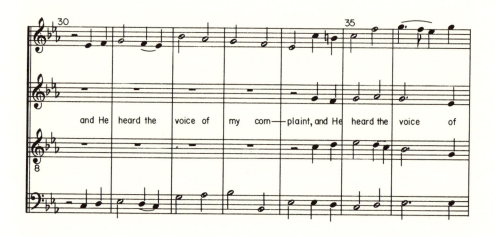

when I was in mi—se—ry He de——li—ver'd me——. Gra—cious is the

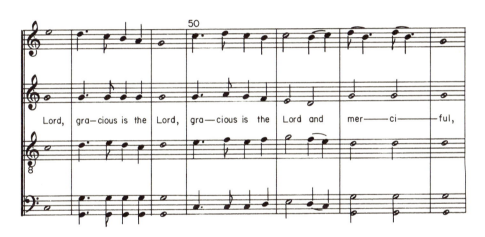

Lord, gra—cious is the Lord, gra—cious is the Lord and mer——ci——ful,

yea our God is a——bun——dant in good—ness, slow to an—ger, for-

-giv—ing i—ni—qui—ty, trans—gres—sions and sin.   Bles—sed be the Lord

God of Is—ra—el from this time forth for—e—ver, from this time forth for—e—ver, from   for-

-e——ver——more,   from   this   time....

this time forth for—e—ver, for—e—ver, from this time forth for——e—ver, for—

-e——ver——more, from this time forth for—e—ver, from this time forth for—

for—e——ver, for—e——ver——more. The

-e—ver, from this time forth, from this time forth, for—e——ver——more. The

for—e——ver, for—e—ver——more. The

for——e——ver, for——e——ver——more. The

grace...

grace of our Lord, Je—sus Christ, be with you all. A——men.

grace...

244

I will love Thee, O Lord

William Billings

love Thee, there—fore I will love Thee, O Lord my strength.

Then the earth did shake ____ and trem—ble. The foun—da—tions

of the hills were re—mov—ed and sha ____ ken be—cause He was wroth.

He bow'd the heav'ns al——so and came down. And dark—ness was

un——der His feet, and dark——ness was un——der His feet.

fly, and did fly ____

And He rode up-on a che—rub, and did fly ____

fly, and did fly ____

—fore I will love Thee, will love Thee, will love Thee, there—fore I will love Thee, O

He de—li–ver'd me from my en—e—mies, and from them which

Lord my strength.

hate me.   for   they...

for   they   were too strong for me.   Then I

for   they...

For they were too   strong,   for   they...

woun-ded them, then I woun-ded them that they were not ab—le to rise.

Then I woun-ded them, then . . .

then they cry'd, cry'd,

Then they cry'd, then they cry'd, then they cry'd, but there was none to

then they cry'd, cry'd, . . .

then they cry'd, . . .

hear them, they cry'd un—to the Lord, they cry'd un—to the Lord, but He

gave them no ans-wer.   Then I tram-pl'd them down, then I tram-pl'd them down, then I

tram-pl'd them un-der my feet.   What shall I ren-der to my God for all His kind-ness

shown? My feet shall vi—sit His a—bode, my songs ad-dress His throne.

Hal———le-lu-jah,   A—

Hal———le-lu-jah,

A—

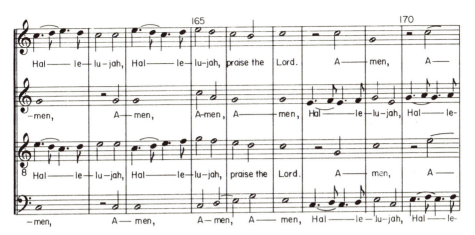

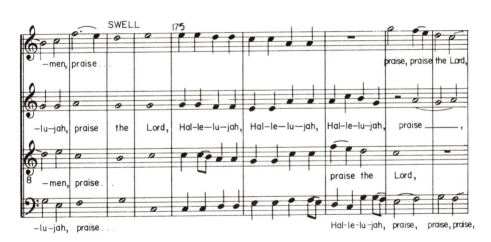

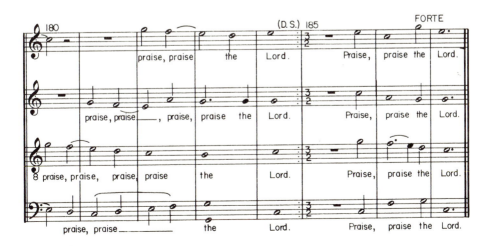

An Anthem

Jacob French

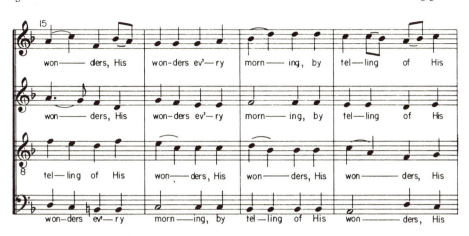

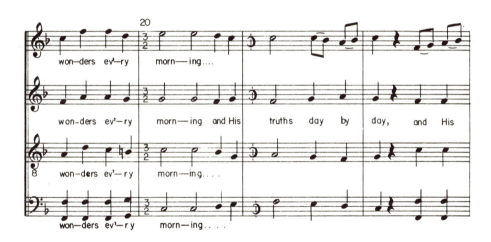

a——bove all gods. Let the heavns re——joice and the earth be

glad, let the sea roar and the full——ness there—of be ——— fore the

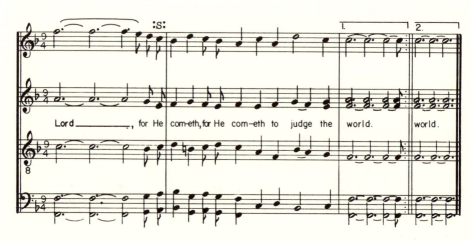

Lord ———————, for He com-eth, for He com-eth to judge the world.   world.

A New Anthem for Thanksgiving

Daniel Read

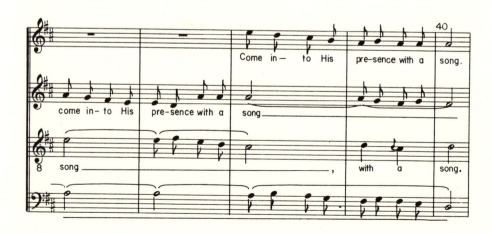

Serve the Lord....

Serve the Lord with glad—ness and come in— to His pre—sence with a song.

Serve the Lord....

Serve the Lord....

ADAGIO

Be ye sure....

Be ye sure that the Lord is God: It is He that hath

Be ye sure....

Be ye sure....

made us, and not we our—selves; we are His peo—ple, and the sheep of His

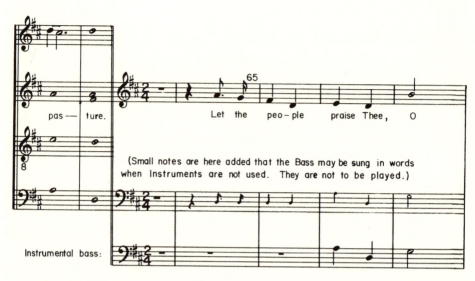

Bles-sed be the Lord God of our sal—va-tion, who

dai—ly load—eth us with His be—ne—fits,

for His

for His mer-cy, His

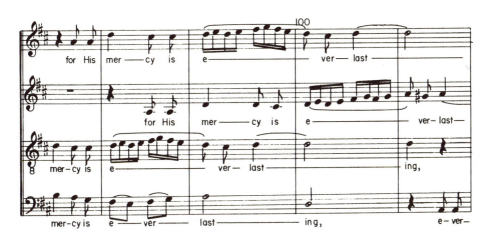

for His mer—cy is e— ver—last—

for His mer—cy is e— ver-last—

mer-cy is e— ver—last— ing,

mer-cy is e—ver—last— ing, e—ver—

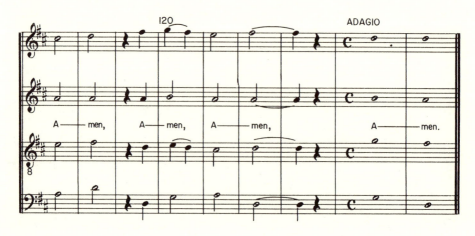

A Concluding Anthem for Thanksgiving Day

Oliver Holden

Counter solo

The eyes of all wait up — on Thee, O Lord,

and Thou gi — vest them their meat in due sea — son.

Repeat the CHORUS

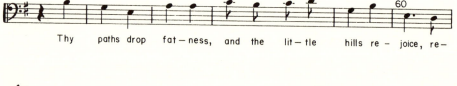

Bass solo

Thy paths drop fat — ness, and the lit — tle hills re — joice, re—

And the lit — tle

joice, and the lit — tle hills re — joice, re — joice

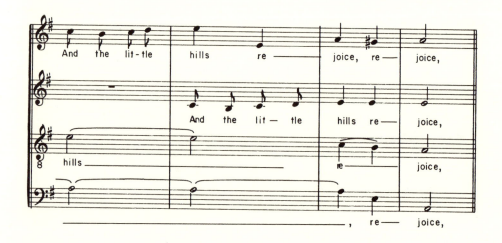

And the lit — tle hills re — joice, re — joice,

And the lit — tle hills re — joice,

hills re — joice,

, re — joice,

Go your way, eat the fat, and drink the sweet, and send por—tions un-to

Go your way, eat the fat, and drink the sweet, and send por—tions un-to

them for whom no-thing is pre— par'd. Hal — le— lu— jah.....

Hal— le— lu— jah, Hal— le—

Hal— le— lu— jah.....

them for whom no-thing is pre— par'd. Hal— le— lu— jah.....

lu— jah, Hal— le— lu— jah, A— men.

An Anthem. Psalm 95, and other Scriptures

Samuel Babcock

O come let us sing, let us sing un—to the Lord

O come let us sing, let us sing un—to the Lord__

O come let us sing, let us sing un—to the Lord__

O come let us sing, O come let us sing, let us sing un—to the Lord__

—, let us make...

—, let us make a joy—ful noise, let us make a joy—ful noise_____,

—, let us make...

—, let us make... let us

we are the peo-ple of His pas- ture. pas- ture. Let us

come be- fore His pre — sence with thanks-giv-ing, and en — ter His

courts with praise, and en — ter His courts with praise.

Ex— alt the Lord our God, and wor—ship at His

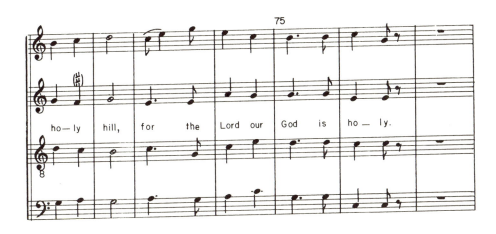

ho—ly hill, for the Lord our God is ho—ly.

for the Lord our God is ho—ly. ho—ly.

Index